". . . the vision of the rational and feeling human being who has the talismanic capacity to look into the darkness and see clearly what is not even visible to others in the daylight."

Harry Mark Petrakis, *Chicago Tribune*

". . . a book about winter in the north woods that ought to do for Clam Lake, Wisconsin, what Thoreau did for Walden Pond. A graceful mixture of observations about humanity, nature, and the poetry of solitude."

Robert W. Wells, *Milwaukee Journal*

". . . this book has a good deal to tell us about the costs involved for a civilization that has lost touch with the feel and rhythm of seasons, the natural cycles of biological life."

Fred Moramarco, *San Diego Reader*

"Move over, Annie Dillard, to make room for a quiet poet who used a winter at his cabin in northern Wisconsin to look at nature and his soul; these short paragraphs and aphorisms have a deeply spiritual undertone or overtone, and anyone who makes use of them will find bases for personal reflection. The next best thing to being in the woods."

The Christian Century

"The book grew out of the intention to 'watch winter,' but its thoughtful and sometimes profound observations define the watcher as much as the natural world he looks upon."

Doris Grumbach, *New York Times Book Review*

The Clam Lake Papers

As scientific understanding has grown, so our world has become dehumanized. Man feels himself isolated in the cosmos, because he is no longer involved in nature and has lost his emotional "unconscious identity" with natural phenomena. . . . Thunder is no longer the voice of an angry god, nor is lightning his avenging missile. No river contains a spirit, no tree is the life principle of a man, no snake the embodiment of wisdom, no mountain cave the home of a great demon. No voices now speak to man from stones, plants, and animals, nor does he speak to them believing they can hear. His contact with nature has gone, and with it has gone the profound emotional energy that this symbolic connection supplied.

—CARL G. JUNG, *Man and His Symbols*

That impulse toward the formation of metaphors, that fundamental impulse of man, which we cannot reason away for one moment—for thereby we should reason away man himself.

—FRIEDRICH NIETZSCHE,
"Truth and Falsity in
an Ultramoral Sense"

Clam Lake, in Ashland County about twenty miles west of Glidden, and on Highway 77, has large muskies. They have access to this lake via the Chippewa River. Not too many good ones are taken here, but occasionally a creditable specimen is landed.

—BERT CLAFLIN, *Muskie Fishing*

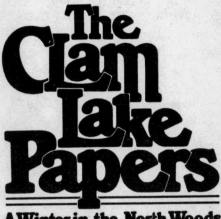

The Clam Lake Papers

A Winter in the North Woods

Introducing The Metaphorical
Imperative and Kindred Matters
With a Prologue and Epilogue by

Edward Lueders

* * * *

Abingdon / Nashville

THE CLAM LAKE PAPERS:
A WINTER IN THE NORTH WOODS

A Festival Book

Copyright © 1977 by Edward Lueders

Festival edition published by Abingdon, May 1982, by arrangement
with Harper & Row, Publishers, Inc.

ISBN 0-687-08580-2

(previously published by Harper & Row under ISBN 0-06-065312-4)

Printed in the United States of America

For Joel

CONTENTS

PROLOGUE

There are still people who confuse individualism and the cult of one's own personality. They are talking about two different things: social and metaphysical reality.

—ALBERT CAMUS, *Notebooks 1935–1942*

Acting a role, realizing in an especially intense way one's identity (in a sense) with someone who (in another sense) one is not, remains one of the most human things a man can do.

—WALTER J. ONG, *The Barbarian Within*

The exquisite truth is to know that it is a fiction and that you believe in it willingly. —WALLACE STEVENS, *Adagia*

Such was my scheme for keeping my second self invisible. Nothing better could be contrived under the circumstances. And there we sat; I at my writing desk ready to appear busy with some papers, he behind me, out of sight of the door.

—JOSEPH CONRAD, "The Secret Sharer"

PROLOGUE

I

I have a summer cabin near Clam Lake, Wisconsin. That fact is basic to everything that follows. For nine months of the year I am a university professor. Customarily, the three remaining months, which allow me time for study and a retreat to the self, coincide with the summer vacation of students. In an older, agrarian society, this made sense. During the summer, all hands worked together to cultivate the earth—to produce the food that would sustain their society through the months ahead. Even today, we consider the cultivation of the earth and the cultivation of the mind as two different things, but custom usually lags behind the times. In the new calendar of humankind, who is to say which is the growing season?

In any event, I am pleased to introduce myself as the editor of this book. What we read—often the fact that we have it in print to read at all—can be said to depend as much on the editor as the author. Ideally, though, I must admit it is the former and not the latter who is unknown. Ordinarily, the editor's task is to blend into the landscape of the work he or she edits, to disappear in the co-accomplishment of the author's best purpose. Whether or not this is finally the case in these pages, the reader is free to speculate. I am afraid I have come to take it for granted.

In this case an author who needed to write got to do so because I provided him the place and proper circumstances, along with the kind of open time and splendid isolation I never seem to manage for myself—a winter at Clam Lake, in which he could follow his concerns wherever they might lead. What later fell to me, was the opportunity to edit his work for publication, for I chose not to have these Clam Lake Papers dismembered, scattered, and interred as if they were Dead Sea Scrolls.

II

Clam Lake lies in northern Wisconsin about midway on the blacktop highway that runs east and west through wide stretches of the Chequamegon National Forest between the towns of Glidden and Hayward. County roads branching off in the vicinity of Clam Lake lead northwest to the resort area of Namekagon and northeast to the lumber-mill town of Mellen.

All these points on the map are set deep in the north-woods country, dominated by forests of pine, birch, oak, and maple, which throw into cool shade the ferny paths along which the deer, porcupine, fox, woodchuck, raccoon, skunk, and an occasional rambling black bear make their way.

In late spring, clusters of flowers in the sparse sections of the forest and along the margins of the many lakes and clearings show where by late August or early September a harvest of wild berries can be gathered. Fat blackberries sprout from spikey branches, and, closer to the ground, one can find their plumper, juicier cousins, the dewberries. Growing in sandier slants of earth, where they can be exposed to much of the day's sun, are the red raspberries, whiskery and benign, ready when ripe to fall into the hand at the gentlest nudging. Along the shoreline of the blue lakes or near the spongy clumps of muskeg in the marshes, the pale blueberries grow.

In between are the ripening days of the short Clam Lake summer. Hot sun and mild, benevolent air alternate with sudden driving thunderstorms that soak the woods and fill the low-lying marshfields. Moods of summer ease and leisure fill the long days before the deep forest green turns orange in the sun's departing light and the night moisture begins to rise to the nightly chorus of insects and the punctuating croak of frogs.

To me, the town of Clam Lake has always seemed singularly well named. It is a graceless, straightforward, unself-conscious name. That part of us conditioned by the promotional language of advertising recoils and scarcely knows how to take such directness. Alongside the pretensions of real estate developers' mellifluous, high-toned names for instant communities, Clam Lake would clearly be an ugly duckling. But I grow tired of Glenwood Acres, Sunnymead Estates, and Lake Olympus Manors, and I respond with delight to the unblinking, forthright spondee of *Clam Lake*. Something totally ingenuous and unexpected lies in the name, but nothing lurks there. It is as tight and open-faced as a $2.98 watch.

Clam Lake is not a misnomer. The area lakes—and there are a number of them connected by the meandering branches of the Chippewa River—all have their bottoms pock-marked by fresh-water clams of no great size. They are unpalatable, according to the natives, and their shells are thin. The creature that inhabits them is vulnerable. Along the shorelines of the lakes you will come across piles of open and shattered clam shells, reflecting brightly through the shallow water, where the stiff-legged herons have collected them to feed upon. When you pick a live one suddenly out of its natural position, stuck vertically into the sandy lake bottom, a wedge of its tough pale white meat will be out. As you hold it in the alien air, you can watch it contract and disappear, like a slowly receding tongue, between the closing halves of its shell. Occasionally this mucous retreat will produce an air bubble—the equivalent, I used to think when I was younger and more romantic about such things, of the accidental pearl in an oyster.

It is the foot of the clam I watch, isn't it? The member on which it moves and the part that probes the lake floor for the organic material it ingests? But is it also then the mouth through which it feeds? Since I have only the most offhand knowledge of clam anatomy, it pleases me to suppose that my Clam Lake clam depends for his very day-to-day existence on his ability to put his foot in his mouth.

Clam Lake. The two words contain such curious contradictions of benevolence and indifference. The flat, hard, basic, biological, almost motionless presence of *clam.* The inviting, rhythmically shifting, salubrious, liquid suggestion of *lake.* The patient, dumb, eyeless probing at the bottom of things in one. The perpetually murmuring, evaporating, sun-reflecting surface-play in the other.

The town of Clam Lake is less ambiguous. The sign on the highway says CLAM LAKE UNINCORPORATED. That is accurate, for the town has no body to speak of, no bulk. Two filling stations, their windows hung with fishing tackle and cards containing gimmicks and gear for transient sportsmen, oppose each other at the east end. Next, a low rectangular building situated lengthwise along the road is identified by an unpretentious sign along the spine of its roof: CLAM LAKE POST OFFICE 54517. Next door is a two-story building that could be taken for a residence except for a small sign over the porch: CHIPPEWA TAVERN—PACKAGE GOODS. At the western end, where the road curves slightly to the south, stands a western-style, flat-front building fortified by gray slate weatherproofing: CLAM LAKE COMMUNITY STORE. The more casual summer tourists may slow down enough to crane their necks and ogle this curious settlement that has momentarily interrupted their green passage through long stretches of woods, but most drive grimly through, barely reducing their speed.

The mail car arrives at the Clam Lake Post Office from Glidden around 10:00, then continues to the end of its route while "Dodo" Dumanch, the postmaster, sorts incoming mail into the rented boxes and prepares the outgoing sacks for pickup and return to Glidden at 11:00. As a result, the town is suffused with people for an hour or so each week day. They meet in the small vestibule of the post office as the mail is going up, or in the tavern, or—most likely at this morning hour—in the aisles of the Community Store where they do their daily shopping, pausing to trade pleasantries and accounts of yesterday's fishing exploits.

By 11:30 the summer residents have returned to their cabins and cottages scattered around the perimeters of the many lakes in the area, and the town is back at its normal ebb. Only an occasional car purrs through as the hot summer sun, its rays now direct upon the asphalt road and the cluster of buildings in Clam Lake Unincorporated, takes dominion over the lengthening hours of the day.

The winter, of course, is another matter altogether. The snows come early, pile deep, and stay late. The stinging cold sets in, drops to zero and below, and remains for weeks at a time. Yet the cold of a Clam Lake winter, except during winds and the worst storms, is not fierce or malevolent but dry, crisp, and clean. The quiet of the snowbound woods is intense, and the open whiteness of the world outside, stuck with hardy evergreens, the black trunks of the oaks and maples, and the peeling gray-white birches, concentrates the warmth and the excitement of life in the human bloodstream, the beating heart, and the active mind.

After the summer residents have returned to central

heating and their city selves, those who remain in this snowshoe and firelog winter busy themselves as they may. Snowplows keep the key highways open with dogged effort, yielding only during the most severe storms, which for short periods defeat all efforts and seal off the sparse north-woods communities from one another. Even in such dark and solitary times, however, television from Duluth and Superior, some eighty miles to the northwest, continues undaunted. Every hearth in winter-bound Clam Lake counterpoints the warm orange flicker of burning logs in the fireplace against the cold electronic flicker of the TV screen beside it. Nowadays, the world may remain physically remote from the winter resident of such an isolated reach of the nation, but not from a sense of the day's events or the civilization to which he or she continues to belong. The length of view increases in the individual as it does in the woods, now stripped of all foliage. The personal world slows down to a walk, and the rest of the world plunges ahead at its usual pace. Through all this, the mind is affected, not so much by its sense of isolation as by its sense of displacement. For months out of the calendar year there is rather little one can do outside. What one does, then, is done inside.

III

My place at Clam Lake is a few miles from town, tucked away by itself on one of the neighboring lakes. The dirt road leading to the cabin is rough, narrow, and winding—long enough to discourage nearly anyone who hasn't been over it and doesn't know what awaits at the far end. Every few years I have to call Buck Metcalf to come over with his bulldozer and reclaim my road from the encroaching woods and the erosive process of winter freeze, spring thaw, and summer downpour. Surging and backing and plunging as he throws the gears and throttles the roaring engine of his straining yellow machine, he bullies the huge glacial rocks out of the roadbed and pushes back the woods. Even then, a few weeks later the road is again in ruts and weeds, won back effortlessly, despite Buck's slashing attack on its bed, by the inexorable will of the forest, reclaiming its own through time and the organic persistence inherent in the cycles of the fertile earth.

At the end of the road sits my cabin, half-concealed in a profusion of pine and birch, on a small rise up from the lake. The construction is of pine logs cut not many miles away and dragged across the winter snow and the frozen lake to the site where building was begun in the spring.

Inside, the cabin is dominated by a huge stone fireplace that covers most of the west wall and tapers slightly as it passes through the steeply pitched roof. When a fire is kept burning for any length of time, the whole rock surface begins to radiate warmth into the room.

Except for one large window, which I added a few years ago to provide a constant view of the woods and lake, the windows are rather small and set in casements six or seven feet above the floor. The main room of the cabin, then, although it is spacious under its pitched roof slanting sharply up to the long lodge pole at its peak, is rather dark except when it is lighted from within. Then the surface of the natural pine logs comes to life, and the whole interior sympathetically reflects the warm light.

In the basement is a small gas furnace, which, along with the stove in the kitchen, draws fuel from a fat, torpedo-shaped tank outside.

On the shelves under the windows and around the walls, I have arranged an excellent library made up chiefly of literature, anthologies, and reference books. In addition, my Clam Lake cabin has become a repository for magazines. Since I seldom have time to do more than glance over their contents when they first come to hand, I put them aside to take up to Clam Lake on the theory that I may browse through them during the summer months. And occasionally, during a rainy spell at the cabin, I will do just that.

When electricity came to the area in the fifties, Joe Renzelmann, Clam Lake's man of many skills, came out and wired the place. Electric appliances of many kinds followed, and their convenience quickly offset any reluctance I felt at seeing the world of muscle and mechanics give way to the age of electricity. One year even the radio had to yield to a successor: I installed a television set, its slender antenna moored to the stone chimney outside and sticking rigidly up over the swaying tops of the trees. With this the transition seemed complete; yet the whole process left my cabin basically unchanged in appeal and naturalness. Life there was not so much transformed by these contemporary devices as it was quickened by them.

More than once I have been caught by the prospect of my edition of Henry David Thoreau on its split-log shelf overlooking the corner that is now dominated by the TV set. Diagonally across from the set is the window that looks out through the trees to the lake. I find I am more bemused than dismayed by living in a Walden wired for electricity. I fancy Henry Thoreau himself would agree, that is, the Henry Thoreau who left his idyllic experiment in the woods after two years because, as he put it, "the universe is wider than our view of it" and he had "several more lives to live."

IV

The Papers themselves were composed, presumably, during the winter of 1969–70. They awaited me, so to speak, the following June when I arrived for my annual retreat and opened up the place for the summer.

Nothing on the outside hinted at any difference. The gates at the entrance to my road were properly padlocked. The road itself had disappeared beneath an undisturbed spring growth of grass and weeds. At the cabin, the crude storm door I had made out of rough boards was in place and secured, as was the covering for the large window, which at closing time each fall I wedge firmly into place over the vulnerable pane of glass. As I removed the storm door and turned the key in the lock of the inner log-door, I felt the quiet excitement that I reexperience each summer when I enter those precincts of my self that have lain inviolate through the deep winter, awaiting my returning step and breath and touch.

My first thought when I swung open the door was disappointment with myself. The great oak table in the middle of the room was covered with piles of papers and green-covered spiral notebooks. These materials were all *arranged*, but even so, they gave me an immediate impression of profusion. How could I have left my table in such a state? It was not in complete disorder, mind you; yet the materials had a familiar aspect of process which on first impression seemed, naturally enough, to be my own.

With curious excitement, I strode past the table and into the kitchen. The dishes were intact on the shelves, utensils hanging in place, cannisters in proper sequence in their rows. I turned and walked through the kitchen doorway, around the corner, and into the bedroom. The bed was made, the dresser top was in order—but somehow it seemed not to be *my* order. I went on to the porch. There was slight disorder there, but certainly nothing disturbing. The stacks of magazines were a bit askew. A copy of *Harper's* lay in the middle of the porch cot. I squinted into the bright June sunlight flooding the porch, then turned and stepped back to the doorway of the main room. I stood there a moment, letting my eyes adjust once again to the small light inside.

My opening rituals had been interrupted, but some routine matters held priority. I went downstairs to the basement, where I threw the main switch and reinstated electrical power. I then started the water pump, which obligingly caught and began filling the tank at first priming, something it had not done for years. Returning upstairs, I undertook a more systematic inspection of the cabin and its contents.

The kitchen was clean and neat enough although some pots and pans were not in their right places. I investigated the cannisters in which I usually keep not only staples such as flour, sugar, and coffee but also a variety of dehydrated foods, spaghetti, crackers, and the like. The containers were either empty or nearly empty.

My property had obviously been used, but without exception it had been cared for conscientiously. Assured, I finally turned to the materials on the table. Beyond questions about the past winter I would ask discreetly around the town of Clam Lake, I kept the matter of an unknown visitor to myself until I had thoroughly considered and studied the materials he had left behind, the Papers that eventually found their way into this volume.

V

To close out my editorial account, I should perhaps explain two features of my arrangement and presentation that otherwise might appear more arbitrary than they in fact are. First, certain books on my Clam Lake shelves revealed boldly underlined passages that I had no recollection of ever having read. The marks had apparently been made by a hand other than my own. From these I have selected, as seemed appropriate, the quotations that serve as epigraphs to the various divisions. Second, among the manuscripts on the table I discovered three letters, clearly penned at different times but each addressed by name to me. I have introduced these letters at intervals sequentially. These letters provide the only formal, direct link between author and editor, and thus between the creation and the publication—what I think of as the maintenance—of *The Clam Lake Papers.*

EDWARD LUEDERS

14

THE CLAM LAKE PAPERS

Part I

But the primitive metaphors do not spring from arbitrary subjective processes. They are possible only because they follow objective lines of relations in nature herself. Relations are more real and more important than the things which they relate.

—ERNEST FENOLLOSA,
"The Chinese Written Character
As a Medium for Poetry"

The ecological complexities of existence overwhelm the human mind, even though some of that richness is an integral part of man's own nature. It is only by isolating some little part of that existence for a short time that it can be momentarily grasped: we learn only from samples.

—LEWIS MUMFORD, *The Pentagon of Power*

There are some enterprises in which a careful disorderliness is the true method.

—HERMAN MELVILLE, *Moby Dick*

Dear Professor Lueders,

It is obvious that you don't use your cabin in the winter, and it seems well suited to my current needs, so I am going to assume your indulgence. I am going to use your cabin for a while, while you are not using it. It is not a matter of money. Nothing, eventually, is a matter of money. I don't have much money at the moment, but that isn't it. It is just a matter of trying it alone somewhere for a while. I suppose I am breaking a law. I am trespassing. But I am also following a law, one printed on the genes and the nervous system rather than in books.

I have some conscience about using your property, but I have owned things too, and I have let people use them. I have let people use me too, as I must have used them. There are balances, I can assure you.

Anyway, by the time you read this I will be gone. You will see that it is not in me to abuse your cabin or your belongings. It took great ingenuity to get in here, by the way, without doing some violence to your property. But I enjoyed the challenge—you went to such lengths to keep the elements and the likes of me out. Ingenuity I have plenty of. Too much. That's part of my trouble. It may take more than ingenuity, though, for you to figure out how I got in. I hope you won't even bother to try. Better just to take me for granted.

I mean no harm. I will use your place, not abuse it. I do not want to thank you for its use, but I thank you all the same. What I mean is, I do not wish to be forgiven. I don't think I need to be forgiven, but I won't go into that. If I am right in my motives, I have some business here or, rather, a need to be apart from business anywhere else—to balance out an account or two. If nothing else, I should have myself to myself for a spell, with insulation. The season seems right.

I know already that I will not get rid of you during my stay unless I take over your property rather than just using it, and I won't do that. Since I will have to accept you this way, maybe it will be easier for you to accept my having been here. No matter. The thing will have been accomplished, and then it won't make much difference, will it?

Here I sit, watching winter. If I so much as stir or blink, the snow and the woods and the stillness mock me, but they also confirm me. While the world outside freezes over and sleeps, I come more and more to life. My every movement grows vivid. My mind jumps and leaps and dances. The world is focused on my next pulsebeat, my next movement, my next thought. In this cold solitude, I am not only sharply aware that I am living; I am even more excitingly aware that I am life.

Marvelous smooth pine logs in this cabin. Cured by time. They hardly taper at all over their length. They fit so well, with their tongues overlapping at the corners. So straight for logs, yet so nicely imperfect in their sculpturing—so unlike the flat, rectangular, plastered walls and ceilings in those unyielding box-rooms we've become accustomed to.

I think I'll rewrite the story about the Three Little Pigs. This time we'll go with the one who built his house out of sticks. Wood, at any rate. I don't recall that the original said how big the sticks were. We'll make them pine, of course, and we'll give him a stone fireplace. No bricks.

Most of the American dream still follows the sun westward to the shores of the Pacific. "Summertime"—as the lyrics of the langorous Gershwin song have it—"and the livin' is easy." But the weather up and down the glamorous California coast is often damp and chill. San Francisco is nearly always damp and chill. Californians don't realize how much of their lives is spent in fog.

I'll take my Clam Lake winter—at least this year. The sun is a marvel, and the air is dry-cleaned. On days like this there is no such thing as a chill here. There is cold, and there is warmth. These are the polar contrasts, and I am in the middle, containing and attesting to both. There is this astounding clarity. No dampness. Either sharp dry or melted into water. No chill. Either cold or warm. I—and not the elements—am compounded of both.

Words. Good Lord. Words.
In the beginning was the Word.
Then came the letters.
Then came variety, diversion, assembly—the words.
Then came the sentence.

Cover a thought before it evaporates. Write it down. Get it right. Get it write.

20

No more than a week, surely, but I've lost track. Is it Wednesday or Thursday? No matter. The sets of days—the gears and cogs of the seven-day week—have slipped already. Amazing. Do I feel like Saturday? Saturday it is. Tomorrow I think I will make Tuesday. Better—tomorrow will simply be the day after today, which will make it also today in its turn. In *my* turn. Each day beginning without a label, ready to develop its own character over its one-time span of hours.

No clock to measure and count off the hours. Good. The hours may measure me for a change.

The sound of the typewriter is the only machine sound I hear. Natural enough to me, clacking out the letters that form the words that become hard exterior statements of my soft interior thoughts. Unnatural, though, against the long, deep layers of soundlessness that surround it, reaching from this quiet, solitary cabin out through the still, stripped woods.

How far away can this uneven, intrusive clacking be heard before it is absorbed and becomes one with the snow, the hard trees, the impartial air?

What feet walked this land before the Chippewa? My boot soles and snowshoes print themselves, not only on top of this winter's snow, but also on top of an accumulation of centuries of steps—back over the countless comings and goings of Earth's animal life, back to the saber-tooth and the woolly mammoth and beyond. Time and motion. Then and now. Back and forth. Creative evolution. *Creation. Creature.*

chickadees	red squirrel
rose-breasted nuthatch	gray squirrel
white-breasted nuthatch	deer (Virginia)
juncos	beavers
ravens	bear (?)
blue jays (noisy)	mink (weasel?)
Canada jays (not)	fox (red)
woodpeckers	otters
downy? hairy?	mink along creeks and rivers
red-headed? red-bellied?	weasel in meadows
grosbeak (evening)	mice
partridge	coyote
owl (great horned?)	rabbit (snowshoe)

Although they've shredded the paper towels—I suppose to pad their nests with—the Clam Lake mice seem to have nibbled at only one book in the whole cabin—the old cookbook in the kitchen. The pages of recipes must have been flipped with greasy fingers.

My fingers always smell reassuringly like me—plus what I've been doing.

In solitude I become sociable and candid. I converse quite successfully.

The language in my mouth
The language in my heart
The language in my mind
The language in my ears
The language through my body
The language through my hands

Much that goes unspoken has its form buried
somewhere in the language, pressing for utterance.
Soundless, I am full of words. Once uttered, the words are
full of me.

If I keep it up, where will it go? What concerns seek
me? The problem: Along what paths will my wondering take
me if I have simplified my day-to-day life enough to let it go
its own "inevitable" way? What concerns will instruct my
thought? What thoughts will construct my concerns? What
subjects: self? survival? sex? religion? reality? Side show or
main tent? How abstract will it become? On what images
will it feed? Big question: In idleness, will thought become
idle?

Alone in this cabin, in these woods, in this world, day
after day, I realize how seldom the language of
conversational speech is the language of thought. When we
are together, how much we mean, and how little we manage
to say.

The wind in the stiff, cold pines and the whistling teakettle on the stove both speak eloquently to me—but not to each other.

I must *say* what I mean, or I may never really know.

Cold is not a force; heat is a force. Cold is what remains when heat leaves. Cold is not active, heat is active. Cold is negative and passive. Heat is positive and aggressive.

But how can I regard the cold in such terms when I open the cabin door or, better, when I shut it against the frozen outside world? I am keeping the warmth in here, but when I shut the door, I firmly believe that it is to keep the malevolent cold out there.

We have a nice expression: "the cold facts."

Such short, swift days Clam Lake gives its winter denizens. It is barely midafternoon, and already the day is fading. The cold twilight takes over the tenuous sky. The winter dark invades, and my lights must go on inside.

Will there ever be reprieve from this brittle, frozen world of snow and ice and stark trees? The idea plays with me that this time no thaw, no spring, no expansive summer will follow; taut, endless winter will go on and on. Through the eons of Earth time, the ice ages come as well as go.

The deer do not inhabit the land in the winter; they inhabit the cold.

What gives a person any worth, anything to go on? The cycle of days and nights proceeds. One sleeps and wakes and sleeps again, but one also eats. One's anatomy functions, one mates. One's acts and thoughts converge, separate, converge, separate.

Our worth is both chemical and mental. We are shaped by our environment, which we in turn shape. We are, all of us, equal parts biology and metaphysics. That is our composition, and the sum is our worth.

Under the smooth white expanse out there lies the frozen lake. From here it could be a meadow in the woods under its deep cover of snow. For a moment I see it that way. Spring has come, and the snow has melted. It is a sun-splashed meadow of waving grasses and wildflowers surrounded by the thick woods.

I see it in my mind for only a moment before it dissolves once again into the rippling lake, reflecting the blue of the summer sky. Then it is again stilled under a solid layer of ice, the ice under its smooth blanket of snow. It cannot be a meadow. The woods would not allow it. Fish are cold and stiff at the bottom, waiting out the confining winter in a narrowing suspension until spring thaws out their sky, opens their world to oxygen and air, and gives them full sense once more.

But for an unfrozen moment it was a meadow. I looked at its white cover of snow, and I saw underneath a meadow.

Tomorrow may be overcast, and I shall be more reasonable. I shall look out and see it as a swamp.

Somewhere within a mile of here a bear sleeps in his cave. I feel it. I sense him there through the Clam Lake winter, dreaming of the Clam Lake summer and the tender spring shoots, the ant-infested tree stumps, the berry patches. . . .

When summer comes, though, will he more likely center his activities in the Clam Lake Dump?

Why shouldn't one talk to oneself? That way one is at least assured of an equal match. Two requirements, though: don't agree too readily and don't talk too loud.

I look at the inside of the log walls, the rounded interior of the logs in the walls. I see the outside of the log walls, the rounded exterior completion of the logs, the weathered side, the rest of the logs that protect me. One projects the other. *I* project the other.

One of my recurring fantasies these days is to visualize the summer woods of Clam Lake submerged somehow within the deep winter freeze. In particular, for some reason, I conjure up the berry patches in their secret summer spots. Those scenes are now so still, so lifeless, so monochromatic in their whites, blacks, and grays. But the berry seeds are out there, solid and stiff in the matrix of the frozen earth where they dropped at summer's end, overripe with the rich liquor of their own fermentation. In time, with the first thaw, they will begin again to yearn, and there will be the sweet berries I visualize, again, in time.

Without other humans to talk to, a man speaks to whatever surrounds him, to whatever may gain his special attention during explicit silences. Sometimes I talk back to the noisy jays or the croaking ravens, but these exchanges are verbal and at their request. The best conversations take place during moments of mute exchange with chance companions that come into sudden focus: the print of snow left by my boot's tread; the pale sun outlined behind the thin veil of a high winter overcast; the sharp diagonal line of the roof slanted against that same sky; an isolated pair of dead oak leaves still clinging to their parent tree and their frail memory of summer; the body of my dissolving breath defined for a moment as I exhale in the cold air; the unseen needles that suddenly scratch at my cheek as I brush past an otherwise still and silent pine.

As I expand by a warm fire inside, everything outside contracts in the deep cold. Some things crack.

In this cabin the television is a curious, alien thing, with its programs packaged neatly in hour and half-hour boxes. At times I find myself yielding to the two-dimensional screen during some electronic Punch and Judy show as if *it* is the reality, as if this cabin and I are in some negligible corner of *its* world instead of the TV picture being in a normally dark corner of ours.

How much and how persistently the choices of our complex civilization usurp the power of a person's native imagination. Our images are all precooked and served up by the public media-mills to suit the most common taste.

The prevailing idea of an *image* in the jargon of advertising and public relations may follow from the growing domination of the photographed world over the personally experienced world. Publicity aims at developing, not the intrinsic qualities of its subject, but the manipulated, simplified, *exposed* image which is to be identified with that subject by the public. This image is related in one aspect to the secondhand experience of gossip and in another to the idea of an unchanging sense of reality we accept in the static two-dimensional photograph.

How inane the commercial world becomes when I myself am neither buying nor selling. "Time is money" becomes the narrowest and finally the most deceitful metaphor I can think of. I wonder how it would translate into, say, Swahili or Navaho.

We are tricked by metaphors from cradle to grave, yet our best insights are caught in metaphors. Something curious there. Something basic, no doubt.

This morning I had a staring contest with the snowshoe rabbit whose tracks I've been seeing around the woodpile. I was cradling an armful of logs to bring in, and there he was, loping toward me from the edge of the woods. I straightened up and froze. He hunched down and froze. We regarded each other for a length of lively moments although the only motion within our mutual fix was the slight twitching of his nose and the silent racing of my brain. I was intent on him, thinking *rabbit* wordlessly, excited by this public/private showing of a local character I had often imagined from his tracks.

And what of him, intent on my curious figure? In what image or configuration did I intrude on his world? What were the enormous differences between my image of him and his of me in that small drama, that standoff at the woodpile? Whatever image his senses finally gave him added up to neither fear, undue concern, nor restraint of trade, for to my surprise he was the first to break the stalemate, resuming his lope with only a slight deflection past the woodpile, on into the trees, over a small rise, and out of sight. I watched him all the way, pleased immeasurably to have been read, accepted, and understood in context.

The trunks of the trees in the woods disappear like shafts stuck clean into the cover of snow. No hint of the tangle of roots below ground, which anchor, relate, and confuse them.

How few are the diagonals in a winter scene, and how cleanly they define themselves to the eye. Any tree that is out of plumb seems to be leaning on nothing, as if caught by sudden cold in the midst of a slow fall and frozen there.

Parallel lines do not *need* to meet; they are plainly sympathetic and make a pleasant match. They compare favorably and set up a constant relationship. Let them meet offstage somewhere in the sweet by-and-by if they must; it will not matter. It is our need for such balanced relationships, our eye's trick of playing matchmaker, that counts.

What I write on the typewriter has a different voice than what I write in longhand.

Under two or three feet of surface ice, the Clam Lake fish wait out their current ice age. In frigid disregard and nonchalance they must share the diminishing depths side by side—the perch, the bluegill, the bass, and the malevolent muskellunge. Do their fins move all winter?

A book on the professor's shelf is called *Language in Action.* Too passive. As I write out these thoughts bred in solitude, it seems more and more that language *is* action.

The company of books, thanks to the book companies.

I had nearly forgotten how to relax and let go of the clock, to read and go with a book. What a frantic, nervous, spastic reader I had become, supposing I had no time and fit only for newspaper jerks and magazine medleys. A dash man. No wind for the distance.

The bookshelves of this cabin, I discover, are full of discriminating people—a gallery to my stage. When I am reading, I become their audience. When I am not, they become mine. A pretty fair exchange, either way.

Reading recent history in these winter woods makes a nice counterpoint to reading the synthetic symbols in all these books. Between storms the surface of the snow accumulates a record of all the doings of the local citizens. I read the tracks of the snowshoe rabbit, the coyote, the deer; I check the groovy snowslide on the north bank of the Chippewa River, where the elusive otters I have yet to see in person conduct their winter sports; I study my own curious trails of an earlier round. The days turn the pages. The nights compile chapters and build suspense. The next snowfall concludes the volume.

The nightly news on television, as in the daily newspaper, is recent, I have no doubt, but it is not as much *current* as it is *arrested* and *static*. What the news media gives us is not "what is going on" but rather a disconnected assortment of separate events, which, having already happened, cannot in any strict sense be "current." I get more of "what is going on"—that is, "what is continuing"—from these books written years and centuries ago than I do from the daily news reports. Nevertheless, I slip a marker in my current book every night and turn on the TV when it's time for the late news.

A moment ago, while reading, I heard a coyote yelp and howl, perhaps a half-mile off in the woods. Then another picked it up, and still another. I wanted with a sudden desperate excitement to answer. I knew the language in my lungs, but my tongue got in its way.

Stones showing in the fireplace:
1. 294
2. 309
3.

The fireplace is insatiable, ravenous. It is a beast I must feed steadily to keep its energies alive and leaping. I'm glad the woodpile is stacked high. I'll have to add to it now and then to keep it looking healthy. At the rate the logs go, I'll have to do it for survival.

How did the Indians ever keep warm through these long winters? Between their constant need for firewood and the beavers' need for food and lodging, it's a wonder there were any trees left in these woods by spring.

A synonym for *economy*, please. All right: *waste*.

When I imagine our world back far enough, I can suppose a time, before people, when animate and inanimate existence on our planet remained well within the natural patterns of production and consumption. Everything took place within the operations of natural supply and demand, of natural cause and effect, of cycles that simply took their own time. Nothing was wasted. Everything, in its own time and function according to the evolving economy of the natural world, was *used*.

33

Economics started with people, not—as might be too easily assumed—because they could foresee needs beyond the immediate ones and thus stored up against the future (animals, birds, and insects do this), but rather because they began to abstract from experience and to analyze and relate their needs—as well as to undergo them. As a result, they devised ways of using nature's resources that altered their roles in the cycles of natural use. They learned to alter composition, as in, say, fiber made into cloth, or *de*composition, as in burning wood or coal. Since this necessarily disrupted the natural processes and the time cycles of nature, it introduced the fact—and the concept—of waste. The story of civilization, seen from this vantage, can be viewed as the development (maybe I should say the science) of waste.

In our own time, waste has become so prodigious that we are about to be engulfed by it. All our waste (which is like saying all our economy) is the product of human ingenuity, of civilization. Because of our prodigality, waste has become necessary, not only to our civilization and to human life, but (so far as our planet is concerned, at least) to all life.

The irony is that the wastes produced by our civilized ways now threaten to destroy either our economy or us. Probably both. It will take all our human ingenuity to prevent this.

Quiet, heavy snow tonight. After a dull, overcast, characterless day, evening settled over the woods with an almost preternatural stillness. Then the snow began. Almost at once the air was thick with huge, feathery flakes, lowering the layer of quietness through the breathless air and spreading it softly over the ground. Since supper I have sat here by the window, watching, engrossed, the room behind me lit only by the flicker of the whispering logs in the fireplace, now crumbling to embers.

Few scenes in nature coax so elemental a response as a heavy snowfall starting at dusk. There is such understatement in the quiet and the cold and the slow buildup of substantial blue-white mounds that materialize on all surfaces and erase the edges from the exposed world. Rain will drum and pound and soak and run off to collect somewhere at its own mean level, but the snow, without weight or sound, accumulates everywhere and stays. The rain responds to gravity on earth as well as in the air; the snow, only lightly concerned with obeying the downward pull while still in air, *bestows* gravity on earth.

No wonder the easy association of the snowfall with death and peace. Each flake, settling at the end of its free fall and flurry in the air, is lost—and found—in the accumulation on the ground. The earth simply accommodates it wherever it may fall. There is such a soft finality in all this—in all its movement in the air, in its mute indifference, in its gentle smothering and sealing of all the earth's jagged rhythms and irregularities, in the cold, bright, smooth stillness we can anticipate when the next day dawns. *If* the next day dawns.

WINTER SET

The child in me loves
the snow falling
in the dark
outside.

The child in me fears
the snow falling in the dark
outside.

In me the child can know
the snow falling in the dark outside.

The child is
in me.

I am
inside.

At least one biblical miracle is nothing to me. I walk on water every day.

Snowshoes would not work on mud.

One truth: History, when seen in sufficient scope to become evolution, is indifferent to the individual. Another truth: All life is advanced through the living of individual lives. We have no difficulty in accepting both of these, but it takes a metaphorical turn of mind to do it.

A superstition is a mystery made to conform to a rational pattern. A metaphor is two rational patterns made to produce a mystery.

Man has two basic instruments—two models or prototypes of *the infernal machine*. One is the clock. The other is language.

The clock is the mechanism that deals with indifferent duration, or time; language deals with human circumstance. Like all machines, both are merely devices, not eventualities, but by controlling them we suppose we might take the measure of all things. All *technique*—at least all *mental* technique—depends on one or the other: clock = science; language = humanities. In their interplay we sense our reality. In their inadequacies we formulate our inadequacies.

People think of words—of language—as material out of which structures are built, but there is a false analogy at work here. Words and rhetorical units are not the structures but the tools—better yet, the blueprints. Out of language we build ourselves.

In language, analogy expresses the principle of comparison: *He thought over the idea for a while as if he were chewing on it.*

Metaphor expresses the principle of integration: *He chewed on the idea for a while.*

Analogy: My mind is like the cabin I am living in; my
thoughts are like its furnishings.

Metaphor: My mind is the cabin I am living in, furnished by
my thoughts.

A false analogy is a common experience, but I never
heard of a false metaphor—only a strong or a weak one, a
good or a bad one. The metaphor is false to begin with.

The art and process of translating must be much like
the art and process of metaphor. Two languages will have
many differences in structure, vocabulary, and idiom, which
the translator must reconcile as fully as possible. The
translator who goes at the job as a matter of linguistic
mechanics will use analogies between the two languages.
The art of the best translator must be akin to that of the
poet—his or her method will treat two languages in
metaphorical equivalencies.

When we compare ourselves with others, the process is
analogy. When we consider ourselves strictly in relation to
ourselves (that is, when we are to ourselves at once the
subject and the object of the consideration, when we
measure ourselves against ourselves) the process is
metaphor.

We are closer to the sky in winter, but the sky seems more remote from us.

How deadly the winter woods would be without the birds hardy enough to stay—the chickadees flitting and chattering, the grosbeaks' flash of color, the blue jays' sharp call and nerve. What in their makeup determines whether they retreat to the south or stand their ground (or their air) through the cold? The crows, for instance, all left, evidently, when the snow cover came on; their cousins, the huge croaking ravens, stay on.

Nearly every day a conversation of ravens catches me. In the clean white stillness their uncompromising blackness and raucous talk are startling interruptions but welcome animation in the woods. Their vocabulary is limited, but it seems to be growing as I listen in from day to day.

Today a sharply rising wind brought me stumbling back to the cabin from an overextended afternoon hike. I made it as fast as my legs and snowshoes could take me, but I was cold to the bone and doggedly mechanical in my movements before I got inside. In physical terms, motion is generally associated with heat, but this does not hold for the Clam Lake winter wind. With even a slight stirring of wind at these temperatures, what has been a reasonably benign day can turn quickly to stinging cold. Today for the first time I could imagine "freezing to death" as something mortally more real than the conversational phrase that frail old ladies use as they *tsk tsk* and pull a sweater tighter around their shoulders. "A man could freeze to death out there," I heard myself mutter when I finally made it back and shut the door against the force of the wind that had pursued and numbed me. I meant it.

If I push my concerns to their limit, the final metaphor becomes the one that relates life and death and makes them one to (and through) the human mind.

We can *understand* (rather than simply know or acknowledge) the reality of any human life other than our own only by means of metaphor. Short of this, we can know it and accept it—as animals do with one another, I suspect— by way of analogy.

Analogy depends on our recognizing basic differences as we compare. Otherwise there would be no comparison. *Metaphor* depends on our ability to allow difference as the basis upon which sameness—even identity—can be asserted.

The unity in our sense of common humanity, the unity that is not yoked to either time or self, is the unity we understand and validate through the method of metaphor.

The two ways of knowing—reason and intuition, science (metrics) and art (rhythmics)—must work together in response to the *metaphorical imperative* that is at the base of the human method. Maybe there is no truly human understanding without both.

Without the metaphorical imperative in humankind, time is indomitable, for separation is the prime condition. To some existential thinkers, human being is apparently no different from any being except by way of the capacity for awareness of a *state* of being. But such a view does not sufficiently recognize the human *method* of being, which is what distinguishes human life from what we conceive as other life, or, for that matter, from nonlife.

The metabolism of the bear sleeping in a hollowed-out cave under mounds of snow is reduced to a trancelike minimum. This enables him to live through the zero of our Clam Lake winter. My metabolism offsets the same wintry zero by increasing my mental activity—at times to an almost trancelike maximum. Each in our own way, the bear and I respond to the common instinct for survival in a cold world.

Found a great word at the end of the *S*'s in the dictionary: *Syzygy*—"the nearly straight-line configuration of three celestial bodies in a gravitational system." *Syzygy.* Now how is a guy ever going to use *that* word?

The most important thing about the doubleness, the duplicity, of our metaphorical method of dealing with reality is that from the outset it made the human being the first, the only, truly ameliorative animal. Manipulating the world through metaphor allowed a person to accept and deal with the factual level of existence—things as they are—while

41

simultaneously envisioning and working toward another more desirable level of existence. With the advent of human mentality and method, mere animal existence divided into complementary dualities, into what has been and what is, as against what might, or ought, to be. Thus religion, hope, and creative imagination in Earth-life entered with humankind.

It appears that the human being, under the impress of the metaphorical imperative, has never been without the urge to transcend self and lot. Nor, more startlingly, has he or she been without the conviction that if one made the right choices on a wide enough scale, one could do so, at least in part, as a result of will.

The moon has given up the night for a while. In its absence, the stars have become incredibly profuse and vivid. Last night I looked long and deep into the innumerable pinpricks of cold light set in the black canopy of winter sky. Today I awoke to see the sun as a close-up in that same expansive interstellar scene. I am warmed, but the perspective of the night sky remains.

We must learn to see the stars in the daytime.

The firmament does not recognize the revolutions of Earth.

The method of metaphor absorbs me more and more. The simple definition of *metaphor* in the dictionary is so neat, so trimmed, so uninspired:

> met-a-phor: a figure of speech in which one thing is likened to another, different thing by being spoken of as if it were that other; implied comparison, in which a word or phrase ordinarily and primarily used of one thing is applied to another (e.g., screaming headlines, "all the world's a stage"); distinguished from simile.

All right. But what lies behind this is so far-reaching, so basic to our thought and understanding, so mysterious, yet so available. We know what a metaphor is when we consider it as an object, a literary device, a thing. The dictionary definition has to see it that way, but what do we know about metaphor as a process, as a means to meaning? What do we know of how it works? Of why it works? Of what it does? What do we know of what the method of metaphor enables *us* to do?

All human language is rooted in metaphor. We assume the word is the same as the thing although we know it is not. Wisdom comes from knowing the difference between the word and the thing and then being able, for cause, to ignore it.

Except for terms that imitate the sounds they designate—like *buzz* or *hiss*—our words are not similar to the things they represent. Rather, for purposes of clarity of meaning and the directness of our response, they *become* for us the things they represent. The word and its meaning in

43

the actual world merge. Starting with names, the process continues through all the complexities of language. When I say *fire* and point to the fire—as I might do in teaching a child—my purpose is to superimpose the word on the thing it represents. The word *fire* is not like the thing *fire*. The method is not that of the simile, for I draw no analogy between the word and the thing. It is a metaphorical relationship.

There is a crucial difference between *belief* and *faith*. Believing requires the assertive involvement of a person in the act of belief. It follows the method of metaphor. Having faith is more passive. It makes of faith a kind of commodity separate from the person's assertive being. In English we have no verb form for faith. We are unable "to faith." Faith is an object or subject; belief is an act or way.

Like a slumbering white giant waking by degrees, the lake responds to the morning sun after a hard, cold night by rumbling and groaning as it contracts and cracks.

The force is considerable. This morning I even saw little slivers of ice kicked up in this grinding process, and I was reminded of the gigantic earth movements that periodically arrange and rearrange the topography of our planet, of the implacable movement of glaciers chiseling out mountain cirques and lake hollows, inch by inch. What powers give shape to our supernatural natural Earth! And what power resides in our unique ability to conceive of them!

On my rounds this afternoon I saw a woodpecker swoop to the trunk of a large pine tree ahead of me. Immediately he shifted his position to the opposite side of the tree. I could hear drumming as his bill probed the trunk like a small jackhammer; so I knew he was still there and at work. But no matter which way I moved around the tree, trying to get a look at him to learn what kind of woodpecker stayed on with me through the winter in these woods, he would move with me, keeping the trunk always between us.

We played the game for some minutes, the three of us— unidentified woodpecker, indifferent tree, and curious man— a rotating syzygy in the otherwise grave air of the woods, before he darted off again, too quickly for me to see much except the arc of his looping flight.

Every human, coming to know he or she will die, seeks to escape the sense of utter finality that lurks in this knowledge. Religions characteristically propose occult and irrational alternatives to the fear of total loss of self and life. Philosophy characteristically attacks the problem by way of intellectual abstraction and the construction of logical, systematic thought. Science, unless it is willing to risk moving into speculative conjecture and thus become pseudoscience, must ignore the matter; death is factual and statistical, not personal. But perhaps in our approach to the question of immortality, as in our quest for scientific answers, we should look for the simplest solution to the problem. The practical answer, the answer closest to us and in that sense the easiest answer, may prove the most satisfactory and have the clearest validity.

The stripped trees and empty stalks of weeds held

immobile in the settled snow are not the only signs of death in the Clam Lake woods. When my mood directs, I can locate death's signature and image virtually everywhere. I think of the carcasses of animals arrested in every stage of decomposition here and there in the frozen landscape; skeletal remains persist for decades, bones with any semblance of marrow or moisture long since dissipated, bleached jawbones of the herbivorous and the carnivorous— of the eater and the eaten alike—with the teeth still in them. I think of the contribution of organic decay to all the fecundity of the forest yet to come, of the husks of insects still clinging in hollow death to rigid stalks or rugged bark where their former inhabitants abandoned them in their advance to the next stage in their metamorphosis, of feathers splayed in disarray around the place where a bird settled to the earth for the last time.

As a human minority in this community, in this dead of winter, I feel mortality both more and less personally, sharing death as well as life with the other Clam Lake creatures in more equable, even more communal, terms than I ever did with human society, which winter now holds at such a comfortable distance from me.

As humans we have both a biological and sociological existence. In the matrix of the two we live out our lives, conscious always of a past that builds, a present that is the realm of action, and a future that we are at some liberty to help formulate. Our biological future is limited by the necessity of individual death. The future of our society can appear limited in the same way, and we ask, Beyond our individual biological lives, what matters? Yet *some* definition of immortality is needed if we are to avoid turning the awareness of our limitation into a self-destructive sense of futility and annihilation.

Metaphor trades in belief. In the middle of *belief* is *lie*.

When separate events or ideas come together, take up the same space, or occur at the same time—if they become in some terms identical—we call it *coincidence*. We are pleased to regard coincidence as mysterious, fortuitous, remarkable, yet we immediately begin to search for a causal relationship. In the first instance we are following the metaphorical imperative; in the second, the analytical need to explain.

As I sit in my Clam Lake isolation writing this, it is strange and difficult to consider the simultaneity of countless happenings going on elsewhere at this exact instant. One part of my mind refuses to believe there is any present reality besides my own at this precise instant in time, supposing somehow that any other present reality must occupy other time, that it could not be *strictly* simultaneous with my own, that, however slightly, it must precede or follow this solitary, palpable *now* of mine.

We must differentiate for the purpose of analysis among the rhythms of the clock, the rhythms of the heart, and the larger rhythms of cyclical nature, but are these not united, as in metaphor, by the rhythms of the mind—or in the human concept of rhythm itself?

The snow will melt. The barren trees will bud. The stark winter landscape will warm to a spring green and flower into lush summer woods, but how do I know this? How do I *see* this?

I *know* it through analogy with past experience—the history of seasonal change I have lived in and learned about. I *see* it through metaphor—the past and the future superimposed on this cold, frozen, immobile present. The metaphorical imperative does not warm the woods, which must await the turn of the seasons. Neither, in fact, does it warm me, but I am speaking truth when I say it does.

From *chaos* we infer life; through *order* we anticipate death.

"In the dead of night." "In the dead of winter." These expressions seem altogether natural, and on the surface, the Clam Lake woods and much of the life that inhabits them support such expressions. The winter landscape seems dead and dispirited; the winter night, doubly so. Yet the cold is a preserver, and the rampant, wild metabolism of summer in this north-woods country, as I consider it today, is much more often the destroyer. Just as heat is the speeded-up action of molecules and cold is their comparatively calm repose, the frenzy of summer is relieved and complemented by the freeze (the frieze?) of winter. The physical world is composed of molecules, their dance slowed to a frigid minimum in winter. The molecular world does not die but achieves a greater composure. In other words, the decomposition of the organic world is arrested. Slowed down, dormant, apparently inactive, it invites the mind. "The dead of winter" is an inaccurate phrase. "The deliberation of winter" might be better.

To see things in terms of something else without losing sight of the thing itself. To seek the core of sameness, the shared identity. A world in which all is relatedness. Not *order,* which is limited to rationality, but *relatedness.* A world of relativity, with the metaphorical imperative at the active center, relating the parts and their movements.

The simile is a theory; the metaphor is accomplished— like a fact. A successful metaphor is a mutation in the evolution of ideas.

When polar opposites can be brought together through sufficient excitation to the point of interchangeability (a form of identity), the results are galvanic and potentially explosive. Magnetism becoming electricity. Fire and water producing steam. Mutual sexual orgasm. $E = mc^2$.

Einstein's formula is a metaphor in which the element of time has been critically reduced (that is, motion has been critically increased), virtually to the disappearing point.

Matter is thus transmuted into energy. Matter and energy—
two opposing factors through the ages—are now equated,
now vitally related. First expressed in metaphor. Substance
seen (that is, *imagined*—how else can we see it?) as force and
movement.

Two ways to release atomic energy from physical mass:
fusion and fission. Joining and splitting. Much greater
energy is released in the act of joining than in the act of
splitting.

Allegory is metaphor extrapolated, metaphor writ large.
That is the trouble with it. It tends to make the method of
metaphor a complete and coherent system, thus reducing all
to a rational scheme of component metaphors. No wonder it
is associated with earlier times, with people and ideas at the
height of the Middle Ages, for instance, when the mind had
to contend with the growing diversity and worldliness of
human experience, with the destruction of the old order and
no assurance of a coming renaissance. They resorted to
systematic metaphor in order to unify and preserve, to defy
history. They constructed allegorical worlds in the name of
truth.

But today? We recognize that systematic metaphor is a
contradiction in terms, and, for the time being at least, most
people, preferring fact and logic, would suppose allegory is
untenable and out of vogue.

Still, what about the growing interest in science fiction?
There allegory seems to be alive and well. Strange. We no
longer credit allegory as a means of systemizing the past or

he present, but it is evidently a natural vehicle for
projecting the future.

Our most profound seriousness and our most profound
humor spring from the same metaphorical acceptance of
contradictory perceptions: that everything in our experience
portends, that everything *seems*, while at the same time
everything in our experience is isolated and disjointed, with
any meaning being illusory. Nothing *is* what it seems. The
expression of this paradox is found in the seriocomic mode
of the *absurd*, a mode that our metaphysics is just now
catching up with and learning to adapt to.

Here and there in the woods I find huge old tree
stumps, their slow organic decay of decades arrested in the
winter freeze. It is bracing to realize they are the remnants of
the native pine forest of another century when the American
Indians shared the struggle for survival on this same
ground—but on considerably more equal terms—with their
animal kin.

The longer I stay in my Clam Lake outpost, considering
the things of this world and my place in it, the more
authentic I find the Indians' religious faith in unseen
processes, and the better I understand my own. How much
difference is there, after all, between the Indians' animistic
and pantheistic reading of the natural world and our belief
in the unseen workings of molecular chemistry and
subatomic physics within the play of surface realities?

Religious revelation is a case of simultaneous cause and effect, but the trouble with revelation in relation to formal religion is that we always tend to confuse *meaning* with immutable *law*. We do not know how to accept spontaneous order without the supposition of permanence.

The longer I go through my solitary rounds and days here, the more the focus of my activity blends with what seemed at the outset an inhospitable setting. My isolation in this winter fastness presses my consciousness back upon itself. Where human company is concerned (disallowing television and books for the moment), I become a society of one, but the isolation also turns my attention and sentimental attachments outward in new ways. I adapt to a context in which my companions are the warping floorboard, crackling logs, furtive mice scuttling along the shadowed baseboard, idiosyncratically dented saucepans, and chipped coffee mugs. I am joined to the society of sounds that accompany all my movements—the creak and rustle of the mattress and springs greeting me as I lie down each night; the same sounds in a different tone of voice when I lie down on a dreary afternoon for a nap or when, half-awake at best, I turn over heavily in the night; the whistle of the wind at the doorjamb as I kick the clogged snow off my boots, conversing with their thumping against the bottom log; the protests of damp wood thrust into a going fire, hissing in anger and dismay; the liquid, sibilant utterances of soup at a slow boil on the stove, of water pouring into my glass, steaming coffee into my cup; the sharp consonants of the typewriter's clacking response as I fix these very remarks on the page, alternating the open vowel silences between the words with the strokes of the keys.

Beyond the cabin too my sense of society is enlarged rather than diminished in the winter landscape as I come to see and sense an increasing number of its citizens, whether their animation be current or suspended—this tree and that hollow stalk no less conversant with me than the agitated discourse of the blue jay, dusting wisps of snow from a branch overhead as he berates me.

Thanks to these far-out Wisconsin winter circumstances, I become less and less concerned with what is called the Human Condition. At the same time, I grow more and more concerned with the Human Method.

In fact, I doubt there *is* such a thing as the Human Condition. There are humans and there are conditions, and it is our fate and opportunity to meld the two. Our prime concern is the human conditioner. To speak always of the Human Condition is to impose upon us through rhetoric a kind of absolute and unchanging domination by circumstance. To think always of the Human Condition is to treat ourselves as static, in the fashion of scientific data. Surely there is more involved in the equation of our lives. In addition to complication, there is always implication. It's about time we see the difference between studying human life in the laboratory and living human life there.

I assume that humankind—the human being—is instinct with language. I think this is a defensible premise, whether we trust in the inductive hypothesis of the anthropologists or in the poetic pronouncement of the Gospel According to St. John: "In the beginning was the Word, and the Word was with God, and the Word was God." I further suppose, as I find Emerson put it, that "language is fossil poetry," that "every word was once a poem," that "every new relation is a new word," and that "the people fancy they hate poetry, and they are all poets and mystics!"

Instinct is nonanalytical, but is instinct subrational or superrational? Both, and at once. Amen.

Eventually we may come to see science as one of the more limited human devices—limited by the same characteristics that have for centuries now recommended the scientific method as the clear road to truth, that is, its deification of objective precision and its limitation of expression to the abstract forms of number and graph.

Psychologists tend to treat people as if they invented them, or worse, are in the process of inventing them. Sociologists treat them as if they were instant history and had no established value in consequence.

But no matter which way we look—ahead or behind—if we are able to look far enough, evolutionary biology, as the parent of them both, and astronomy, as the expanding container of all our realities, reduce such pettiness to size.

Could pressure be but another form of time? Or could time, to put it another way, be pressure eternally present and being equalized?

Consider the difference between wood and coal burning in the fireplace.

The photograph has revolutionized our image-making habits, but the revolution goes widely unrecognized. Such metaphorical phrases as "to look on the face of God" become ludicrous in the context of a photographed world. In this respect, the poetic image, the mental juncture in metaphor of word and thing, and the figurative expression of a truth become increasingly important to balance for us (maybe I mean to *offset*) the strong claim of the photograph upon our belief, as if it did not also in its way lie.

Sitting motionless here at the table, my thought sometimes runs dry, like the river I've heard about in Nevada that suddenly sinks and disappears, swallowed into an unbroken expanse of desert. For me, though, there is no desert. What fills the void when the thought runs out is an unfathomable richness of silence. Most of my life—with the exception of a few sharply remembered experiences of aloneness as a child—silence has been a matter of duration, a short period between customary sounds. Here at Clam Lake, the silence is more positive than negative, with a dimension of enormous depth as well as duration. Sounds become merely the interruptions in customary silence. When the mock utterance of my thoughts or my written words cease, it is *they* that seem relatively puny and empty. The silence that draws me out and out seems physically present yet limitless in its reach and capacity—perhaps so total in this respect as to be indescribable. I cannot easily say whether I find it comforting or fearsome, for it seems at once to reflect me and to ignore me.

It is a commonplace that time—or duration—is a fourth dimension. Has it been suggested that in human terms this dimension includes death as well as life? The four-dimensional person may be the one whose life-view includes integrally the time both before and after his or her biological existence, not just as simple continuity, but as reconciled opposites.

The process of drawing analogies in the consideration of death-in-life and life-in-death principles only perpetuates our dilemma in trying to grasp and express such matters. The only method that will serve is metaphor.

CONSPIRACY OF SILENCE

Buzzing in my ears, the silence fills
this black, premonitory night. Why not?
That steady hiss is me and my awareness
that a softness somewhere takes its waxen ease

like petals in the dark, relaxing. Well.
I know the things I cannot see within
that strain of sound in me. Without the hum
I have no ear, no sense of now. Eternal

sibilance enables me to furl the flower
and wilt the grass, to flit the bat and share
the rabbit's static fear tonight—
electric and explicit
in the buzzing
in my ear.

There is a nice reciprocal arrangement in certain
sections of the woods between the birch trees and the pines.
In their diversity, they serve one another. The fast-growing
birches thrust their supple trunks above all but the tallest
pines, losing their lower branches as they rise, and
maintaining only the current clusters of their swaying
branches at the top. Meanwhile, year by year, the pines
patiently inch upward, the flexible birches protecting them
from the brunt of windstorms that otherwise might topple
their stiff, straight trunks and bring their neat pyramids of
needled branches prematurely to the forest floor. Where the
birches' protection is absent, I sometimes find pines down
flat from the wind, with their tangle of roots and the layer of
frozen earth in their grasp upended in the air.

In return, when a pine, in outlasting generations of
neighboring birches, does achieve its mature growth and
finally falls from its own age and weight, its massive bulk
will begin the slow process of rot and decay, replenishing
the forest floor over many more years with the rich organic

material from which new generations of birches will take
their nourishment.

I've looked again at the dynamics of these woods, and I
find over-population a problem. Apparently cooperation is
offset by competition throughout the natural world. Neither
trees nor people are exceptional in this respect. As often as
not, birches and pines compete for the same forest ground.
Although stronger and more sturdy, the slow-growing pines
can be inhibited by white birches struggling up too close to
them. During their movement in the wind the birches will
constantly worry the pine, disfiguring it and even destroying
its leader and the tender ends of its branches on which life
and growth depend.

Odd to think of trees in the woods being subject to
diseases—their mumps, measles, malignancies—but of course
they are. The tree has hazards as do we all; yet much of the
life that continues to animate these woods through the hard
winter needs the trees that are in trouble as well as the
healthier ones that furnish browse for the deer, cuttings for
the beaver, nibblings for the rabbit. Without the insects,
larvae, cocoons, and ant eggs lodged under the loose bark of
diseased, infested, and dying trees, chickadees and
nuthatches would have a considerably harder time of it. So
would woodpeckers, although they are equipped to do their
own drilling, if necessary, to expose their grub. The
woodpeckers' nests, like those of squirrels, need the hollows
to be found in trees that have survived and grown around a
diseased or wounded part.

Things become obsolete awfully fast nowadays. It appears that nothing is proof against obsolescence, that nothing is, at last, sacred. At the practical level of our lives, we will just have adapted happily to the use of some everyday product—say laundry soap—when the ads on television and on the package proclaim a new, improved formula.

To move to the spiritual end of this same spectrum, we are encouraged to entertain the idea, along with the New Theologians, that God is dead. Well, why not? If we are going to live with obsolescence, we might as well start at the top.

Obsolescence is a perspective, or attitude, for viewing what, from another perspective, we call *change*. From still another perspective, we call it *growth*. The very cells that are the basis of living tissue are, at any given moment, if you wish to see them that way, obsolescent. For that matter, it is necessary to approach all life as a matter of dying, just as it is necessary to approach all life as a matter of living. I guess the business of theology is to relate these two—the matter of dying and the matter of living—in a satisfactory (and satisfying) way.

The days close in, the snow deepens, and my winter lengthens. The time of sleep for the hibernating bear grows shorter.

The opportunity to be profane—I might even say the *freedom* to be profane—depends entirely on the condition that *something* be held sacred. The opposite is also true.

What we traditionally think of as bad language can be divided into the profane and the obscene. The frame of reference for the profane is set by our religious and vital *spiritual* needs. The frame of reference for the obscene is set by our biological and vital *physical* needs.

Like every society, every tribe, we have our language taboos. We pass along to our young the idea that certain words and expressions are bad language and should not be used, but we rarely go far into the matter of why we think they are bad.

If they are bad, would we be better off without them?

What antique superstition stands behind the notion that *damn* and *hell* are bad words and that *kill* and *murder* are not? Certainly *rape* is a more obscene concept than *fuck*. Why then do we not consider it a more obscene word? Is there something in the extent to which a word has been made flexible in its metaphorical uses that spells the difference?

"Bad" language may be language in which fact and truth are assumed to be forever separate.

Every time I see or hear the word *theology*, which is apparently in vogue again, I feel I must somehow contend with Jehovah, the God of the Christians, evolution, and $E = mc^2$ all in the same instant. I must also juggle antihistorical concepts of totality together with historical and scientific facts of sequence and development. Under these circumstances, I suppose I should be grateful to have the figure of Jesus Christ to help me out; yet Jesus seems blissfully remote from the snowscapes of my Clam Lake winter.

I am struck by my own use of the phrase "the figure of Jesus Christ." The word *figure* is the curious one here.

We too easily assume that Jesus Christ is simply a person's name—like Albert Einstein, Abraham Lincoln, or Pablo Picasso. As a name, Jesus Christ is actually more like Genghis Khan. It is at once a name and a designation, a proper noun followed by a common noun. Maybe we should insert a comma in such names to signal the relationship between the two parts: Genghis, Khan. John, Baptist. Donald, Duck. Jesus, Christ.

To invoke the *name* of Jesus Christ is to imply the comma. To speak of the *figure* of Jesus Christ, on the other hand, is to give—as in the metaphysical clinching of poetic metaphor—equal and simultaneous emphasis to both the person and his significance, to both the natural and the supernatural being.

I read of wife-swapping in the suburbs and of the more public equivalent among show business celebrities. Well, with marital partners up for grabs, that leaves only two commandments standing in regard to fooling around with your friends' possessions. Both are set not in the bedroom or the bathroom, as might be expected in a more circumspect age, but in the living room: (1) Thou shalt not rearrange the fire in another person's fireplace; and (2) thou shalt not adjust the picture on another person's television set. Alas, I trespass on both counts.

One of the arts of imagination lost with the passing of childhood is watching shapes, faces, and figures form in the clouds. Taking advantage of some remarkable midwinter cumuli overhead today, I tried again, but I couldn't stay with it. I saw plenty of shapes form in the drifting clouds, but none registered more than fleetingly as kittens, goats, bears, or rhinos. They all turned into Hogarth caricatures of humans.

The pine tree is neoclassical; the maple is romantic.

One effect of advertising in the United States has been to extend the optimism of nineteenth-century America into a twentieth-century world that would otherwise be hard-put to support it. Optimism in nineteenth-century terms should be bankrupt in ours, but the dominant theme of advertising perpetually redeems it. In the world of advertising, everything is always improving, always becoming better and better, more and more desirable. The greatest satisfactions always lie ahead.

The old expression "time is of the essence" has a final kind of validity that our casual and trivial use of the phrase belies. We are haunted throughout our existence by the exteriority of time. We must recognize always—even if we then go on to discount it—that there is time exterior to us and to our individual lives.

Biologically, we are all involved in transmitting particular forms through evolving time. We call the process *genetics*. In this we are one with the plants and animals, but the great difference between the forms and classes of life in this respect is the absence or presence (and the degree) of *will*—or what I want to call *self-conscious complicity*—in regenerative procedures. That is a long-winded and sterile substitute for what we should mean, but nowadays seldom do, by the word *sex*.

Compassion is possible only as a metaphorical extension of self-knowledge. Else it is at best pity.

There is an unnatural condition in being here. I have no human companion. I neither touch nor share with any other person. Among all the animals in these woods, I am probably the only one who is solitary by choice. It is biologically and psychologically unsound. I console myself that it is only a temporary arrangement, but that does not dissuade my glands and hormones from their regular urgings, nor does it deliver me from my dreams of erotic glory. I should not know myself, though, without them.

At odd moments lately, I have experienced a peculiar split sense of time. On the one hand, I am conscious—comfortably conscious—of the time I consume in all customary activities. I know how long it takes to walk from the kitchen to the porch, to boil a pan of water, to get my clothes on (rapidly) when I get out of bed and into the cold morning cabin air, to hike to the nearest bend of the Chippewa River and back, to coax a fire from match to kindling to full roaring conflagration. Such time I measure with physical movement. As a clock or watch tells time through its "movement," so I tell time through mine—Clam Lake movement rather than Swiss movement, you might say. But there is a second kind of time of which I can become equally aware. It is without specific movement of any sort and hangs in the still air of the woods. It is the space between the trunks of the trees, the time apart from the rhythm of my own breathing. It is tacit, motionless and inert in the frozen earth, the limitless sky.

I flushed a lone partridge out of a deep snowbank not five feet in front of me this morning. The commotion was sudden and startling. The whirr of its wings up through the deep snow and then into the air was as sharp and vibrant as a motorcycle motor. I remember hearing how a partridge will dive from branches into fresh snow to sleep under its insulation. It must be true. At least one other local creature is sleeping alone these nights besides me.

In its metaphysical rather than its physical aspects, time is separable from the biological organisms that inhabit it and reproduce within it. There is always, for humans, an inescapable sense of exterior time beyond us; it is something other than any single life can encompass in fact. In any mortal scheme yet devised, it is also a sense of time distinguished from all terrestrial, substantial life.

To the Hindu, all becomes synonymous in Brahman, a concept in which time, substance, and all cognitive being, *along with their opposites,* become indistinguishable.

The dance of life equals the dance of molecules. All science becomes time-and-motion study. Shall we thank God or humans for rhythm?

What we have thought of and studied as history all these years is considerably less than that. It has been political sequence. At best it has been the history of individuals—that is, biography—but it has not been sufficiently broad, knowing, or extensive enough to be the history of the individual.

Another lie we must believe: one must live as if he or she were at the center of the universe, knowing, of course, that he or she assuredly is not. Life depends on the single self as the focus of all sentience, yet everything living is defined by its dying. No single life is by itself central—or ultimately even necessary—except as it is lived.

Wit depends entirely on flexibilities in language and the possibilities of multiple meaning. Take away the method of metaphor, and we live, quite literally, in a witless world.

Our bond with the earth and the age-old glorification of honest toil are badly in need of reinterpretation.

I find a critic writing callously in *Harper's* about the stories of Hamlin Garland that dealt with the hardships, courage, and economic exploitation of farmers in the north-central plains. His critical point is clear:

> After one reading . . . most readers are through with Garland. He lacks relevancy. Conditions in our rural Midwest have changed, and life for the people there is no longer one of unending toil. Furthermore, his stories, by themselves, contain little to hold our interest. The characters in "Under the Lion's Paw" are a good example of this. They are plain but decent

people who are trying hard to make a life for themselves. They are also colorless bores.

I think this last observation is the most revealing. Work, in the old sense, apparently is not the stuff of life any more. The Eleventh Commandment—or perhaps the First in the New Decalogue—may be taken from the tacit code found in all popular literature from the *New Yorker* to *Mad Magazine*: Thou shalt not be a bore.

There are curious confusions about such items as *labor, work, job, occupation, profession,* and so forth. Under *labor* we have come to include anyone who is employed or employable. The term is applied more and more to people and less and less to what they do.

Something I read this evening called me up suddenly to the fact that I am an American, a creature-citizen of the United States of America. It seemed more like a recollection than a present fact, a condition I have conveniently neglected and all but forgotten.

I feel peculiar and wry about it. I clearly remember being an American, of course, and slip back into the mold easily enough, but it is like putting on an old, once-fashionable suit of clothes after months of nothing but loose woolens and old jeans. Without advising myself, I had come to assume that I was simply a participant and an observer in the principality of these woods—the sole inhabitant of this cabin, perhaps even the principal himself, the leading citizen pro-tem of the nation of Clam Lake. For the moment at least, it's hard to decide which nationality is illusory.

A world view of the spiritual nausea and sickness unto death that is so much a part of twentieth-century life: Asians are born nauseated; Europeans have achieved nausea; and Americans have had nausea thrust upon them.

A mathematical equation is a form of metaphor. It is a neat balance struck between two or more different elements. The precision of mathematics demands the achievement of virtual identity rather than just similarity. The ideal of the equation is complete conversion, interchangeability. Its factors are equal to, not merely like, each other.

I am missing the point too often. It is not the metaphor as a rhetorical phenomenon that intrigues me. It is the process of mind that enables it—demands it—as an essential human tool, maybe *the* essential human tool. But I get tangled in the old problem of substituting the definition of the process for the process being defined.

For example, the mathematical equation itself depends for its truth (as against its mere validity) on the human mind, which, by its movement in metaphor, can bring the two sets of factors in the equation into the realization of their equality, of their oneness. Mathematics itself depends on displaying the *differences* that define and separate the factors of the equation. The human mind represented in the "equals" sign brings the diverse factors effectively *together*. Mathematics, as such, can at best measure differences. The basis of all numbers is rooted in difference. Ultimately, it is the human technique of metaphor that transcends the analogical limits of mathematical manipulation.

The celebrated objectivity of numbers, the vaunted "reality" of arithmetical relationships, the "purity" of mathematics—all these are as finally dubious as the myth that there is safety in numbers. The only difference between mathematics and any other analogical approach to reality is the level and consistency of abstraction involved in the numbers game and in the signs it uses. Mathematical truths, like all truths, depend on the capacity of the comprehending mind to understand through metaphor. After all, any abstraction is, so to speak, a lie.

A person is at his or her best as an architect—at least in the general sense of designing and constructing something that will be inhabited by humans or will in some effective or affective way house their bodies, minds, or souls. Most ideally, all three, together.

Probably the architect is to be distinguished from the builder in his or her integrated concern for all three. To ignore the body is to ignore the common lot and the common sense of humanity. To ignore the mind is to ignore the individual lot and the individual options of each human. To ignore the soul is to ignore the continuing and necessary bond between the other two and thus to deny any meaning

69

to the human enterprise, not only meaning beyond mere utility, but, sooner or later, meaning *in* utility as well.

I wonder if the man who built this cabin worked from a complete set of plans. Did he know before the building began just how it was going to be? Some parts of the cabin must be the result of adjustments or improvisations that happened along the way, but which parts? What problems, decisions and inspirations came up along the way? I have yet to see a finished building that came out just like the architect's drawings. Never mind, the cabin is all one now. It is a good cabin.

Unity through duplicity:

The effect of unity in the human mind is often gained through the coordination of certain dualities in human physiognomy.

Two eyes. Each "sees" a different image; yet the effect is of one image to the interpreting and containing mind.

Two ears. Each "hears" from a different angle and distance. Together they locate or "center" sounds by a kind of instant triangulation.

Two arms and hands. They can be used singly, but they assure our strongest grasp on an object when both are used together, from opposing points of leverage.

Two legs and feet. In ordinary walking they alternate, but they substantiate our sense of balance best when both are used simultaneously. Some popular expressions of this: "to land on both feet," "to have both feet on the ground," "to stand on your own two feet."

The physical basis for the continuity of human life is rooted in biological metaphor: man and woman, distinct and "opposite"—or at least *complementary*—as male and female. The union of complements in the physiological process of procreation produces the new individual—the child. Sex is the metaphor of human generation.

The emotional basis for the continuity of human life is rooted in the metaphor of love. Two beings complement and fulfill each other. The love that most proceeds from duality and difference (heterosexual love, love of parent for child, love of those identifiably different and distinct from one's "own kind," love of one's enemy) is creative. The love that proceeds from unity and sameness (self-love, racial alliance, nationalism) is dedicated to stasis and is, sooner or later, destructive. It is love based on analogy; creative love is based on metaphor.

Paradox brings together two contradictory items that are both reasonable and true. It offers a standoff, a problem. Nothing happens.

Metaphor brings together two items, one of which, for the sake of reason, can be seen as false. It offers a blending, a solution. Something happens.

Smooth to the touch,
My memories of you;
I've handled them so much
No facet can feel new.

Yet every recollection
Holds me like a pledge,
Confounds my intellect and
Hones its cutting edge.

Author-ity moves in mysterious ways. Writers are notoriously egocentric; yet they often testify to a common worship of those stretches of rapid composition when some energy not wholly their own seems to preside, when the course of their expression seems ordained, when they seem to be less author than scribe, less entity than medium. I am beginning to understand what they mean.

The common term for this experience is *inspiration*. Ernest Hemingway, as I recall, spoke of it with respectful understatement as *luck*. Although it is quaintly archaic now and suggests gas on the stomach or a swollen windbag, the accepted term was once "the divine afflatus." The ancient Greek practitioners in the arts and sciences knew what they were about when they called on the muses to take over and guide their work, acknowledging at least co-authorship with the gods. The whole history of what we call revelation, or the creative process, might be invoked to support their point.

Robert Frost wrote that the poem is "a momentary stay against confusion." The fact that it is momentary, that it is an act of language without supernatural belief required beyond that fact, makes the poem especially appropriate to our need for mystery today. It does not require us to treat it as sacred, as a revelation of unalterable truth granted to us from extrahuman sources.

Yet we should remember that throughout history the poetic process has been considered an act of grace. Homer invoked the muse before he undertook his epic poems. When I ventured to coax some verses into being recently, so did I. The idea of inspiration being courted—even worshiped and sacrificed to—has always prevailed in the popular image of the artist at work.

To this extent, at least, it remains true: Even though we are assured that it is the writer who constructs the poem, play, or story, and not a god somehow taking it over, we still require that the work provide us—and deal with—some order of mystery in our lives and in our process of comprehension. We ask of the work some extraordinary rendition of experience, the province of which is not primarily the facts of existence (these belong to the fact-finders, the scientists) but rather the ramparts of the human imagination.

The final discipline the writer learns is not to tell everything he knows. Fortunately, the reverse is not true, or no writer would ever succeed. It is not necessary for him to know everything he tells.

December 24

Dear Edward Lueders,

Christmas Eve, Lueders! It's Christmas Eve in your cabin. We're celebrating, and you don't even know I'm here. Shame.

Edward Lueders. How do you pronounce your name, old boy? Is it **Lewders** or **Leaders**? Two different people in there, you know. Which will it be? Or are you the kind who can have it both ways? I find nothing among your artifacts that tells me, and I spend a lot of time poking around your artifacts these days. And nights.

Would we get along? Maybe it's just this Christmas spirit (you wouldn't deny me that, would you, old boy?), but I think we would, you and me. Tonight, at least, I think we would. You might be pleased to know that I talk to you at times. Some sort of vague rivalry, I suppose. I think it started when I found your electric blanket and realized I could come out from under that monstrous pile of comforters at night. "Lueders, you old bastard," I said, and I liked it.

It's Christmas, Lueders. We ought to be raising a glass together and celebrating. My fire is roaring in your fireplace.

I've just been watching Earl Henton and the news on

channel 3 from Duluth. What a Santa Claus he would make—at the studio Christmas party, maybe. "Merry Christmas, everybody! A family of five from Bemidji were all killed instantly early today when their car was sideswiped by a truck etc., etc." Twinkle, twinkle. "Merrrry Christmas! A widow and her three small children burned to death in their beds early this morning when their unvented gas heater etc., etc." Twinkles again. Slide the glasses down the nose a bit, Earl, and dip your head to peer over them. A little more kindly now, Earl—like you were changing over from the news to a commercial. That's it. Now the Santa Claus beard. Pull it down a shade more. It wiggles too much when you talk and spoils the illusion. Perfect. Now read the news, Earl—or rather the calamity sheet. No one would recognize the news if they heard it. Not even tonight, eh, Lueders? Deck them all with news of folly! Merry Christmas, Earl. Merry Christmas, ev'rybody.

And a Merry Christmas to you, Lueders, and my thanks for your involuntary hospitality. Are you a Christian, Lueders? I suppose you are—as far as your professorship will allow, hmmm? Well, let's think of your permitting me to use the cabin as an act of Christian kindness. Or, since you have so little control over it, think of it as an act of grace. Tonight I would even be willing to call it an act of charity. Why not? I am needy. I admit it. Yes, indeedy, I am needy, not seedy, but needy. We all are needy.

But I want you to know this, Lueders: My spending the winter as your guest here is not so much desperation as inspiration. When I came here, it wasn't because I didn't have anywhere else to go; it was because I didn't have to go anywhere else. I want you to know that I am not indigent,

Lueders. I am needy, but I am no bum. I need to spend some of the winter here and see what things are like, see what I am like, see what it is to see. I can report that it is beginning to work out, old boy. Or to work in.

You'd like it here, Lueders, if you could stand the solitude. Just right for me so far. Solitude leads to amplitude. Still, I talk to you now and then, to hear my voice and to let you in on the deal. I also talk back to the television, a regular running dialogue. Great sport, by the way. It sharpens the flair for repartee, and without opposition. You can win every time. The dolts on the tube plunge ahead no matter how you jibe, counter, insult, or libel them. Commercials are tailor-made for this. It's the secret of their success. All designed to make you feel superior. Talk back. Scoff. Remember the product that way. Insidious.

It's also dreadful to realize that flipping off the switch doesn't stop them. Nothing stops them. They go on and on, all the time. Jabber, jabber. Laughter up, laughter down. Music cues, titles. Dramatic pauses, emotional rush of words. Horses galloping. Another set of horses galloping. Bloody fist-fights every five minutes. Commercials for beer, shampoo, automobiles, detergents, appliances, deodorants, mouthwash, gum, aspirin, living bras, toilet tissue. Commercials interrupting this program to plug another program later—commercials talking to commercials. All there, mixed up, all going on, all day, all night—whether your set is on or off. Distressing thought.

But the snow, Lueders, the snow on television, I mean, as well as the snow outside. Can you imagine my glee the first time it happened? I think it was during the first real storm. Forget what I was watching. No matter—they're all comic strips of one sort or another. The storm grew in intensity, and the interference on the TV increased with it. I glanced out the window over the set and watched the whirling, flurrying flakes. The air was thick with them. Couldn't see any but the closest trees through them. Then I dropped my eyes back to the TV, and, lo, the snow was dancing there too in its dizzying electronic patterns. Horse laugh. Everywhere I looked, snow took over my vision. Covered all images but my own. Covered all over with snow.

Carried away, eh, Lueders? Well, it's Christmas Eve, man. I'm being convivial. Can't spend all the time just thinking my thoughts. Began writing them out a while back. It helps to think a thing out, writing. Find out what you mean. Good habit, writing. Talk it out and it's gone—evaporated. Write it and you've got to think. No alternative. Hard work, writing. Takes time to write it out. Plenty of time to work, to write, here. Nice place you've got. I've got. We've got.

Almost midnight, Lueders. Glad to have you aboard. Hope sometime it's mutual. Merrry Christmas, Lueders, you old bastard. Merry Christmas. Enjoyed the party. Can't wait around for Santa any longer though. Excuse me, old man. Tired. Time to sack out. Got to be ready for the new day.

THE CLAM LAKE PAPERS

Part II

We are the final product of the Pleistocene period's millennial winters, whose origin is still debated. . . . Illiterate man has lost the memory of that vast snowfall from whose depths he has emerged blinking.

—LOREN EISELEY, *The Unexpected Universe*

Nobody has found out that the "material" meaning of every word has actually preceded the "mental" meaning. The opinion that it has is merely based on a presumption—that the physical is *more true and more real* than the mental, and hence that the physical is at the foundation of all things and is the principle of all *explanation*.

—DENIS DE ROUGEMONT, *Love in the Western World*

The human brain is the kernel which the winter itself matures.

—HENRY D. THOREAU, *Journals*

The momentum of the mind is all toward abstraction.

—WALLACE STEVENS, *Adagia*

A strange and memorable experience this morning. A sight I won't forget. The coldest day so far, also the brightest and the clearest. The sky so clear, the sun so intense, the air so cold that all moisture in the air had frozen and drifted in crystals to the earth, where it added a glazed coating to the snow. Humidity and temperature at zero and below. The stillness was apparently absolute. The sun flooded the landscape. Nothing moved.

At midmorning I put on the snowshoes and ventured a half-mile or so into the barren, soundless woods. The noise of my movements—even the rustling of my clothes and the audible rhythm of my careful breathing —became assertive and distinct, became almost substance in the still world.

But the startling sight awaited my return. When I turned back, I saw far above the trees the incredibly long, impossibly straight column of smoke from the fire I had left burning in the fireplace. Without an inch of deviation it rose up and up and up, perfectly true, until it disappeared beyond the reach of my eyes and into the realm of my imagination.

Then, as I came nearer, I could see the chimney from which it issued, but that did not at once make sense. The sequence had been inverted, and for a while I could not shake off the force of the inversion. It started with the far end of that smoke column at the limit of my sight and beyond. Then the perfect, taut rope of smoke descending straight down until it entered the chimney. And finally, as I drew close, the cabin itself at the bottom, at the end of the order. It was as if the cabin and the earth on which it stood in that stark, sun-bleached, mute reach of woods, hung from—I am tempted to say *depended* from—some fixed point in the magnificent still sky beyond my fiercest vision.

An extraordinary effect. It was still with me when I got back inside the cabin and closed out the sky and put on some new logs to revive the fire that had burned down to a steady glow and smoulder in my absence.

Odd that we have become so thoroughly dependent on sight as our access to reality. Do we not feel the way things are? "Seeing is believing" we say. What's wrong with "smelling is believing" or "hearing is believing" or "touching or *feeling* is believing"? Why give the sense of sight such a monopoly on belief? Ah, but it is the image-making process of the mind we are talking about, not the physical sense of sight alone. Doesn't the mental image duplicate and combine all the senses? Isn't the mind of a person involved in the act of seeing? Isn't the mind therefore a part of what one sees?

When did the mental image give its franchise to the picture? To the photograph? A camera doesn't see. A photograph doesn't see. We see the photograph, and we are more than eyes. We are a complex of emotions, experiences, methods, tendencies, awarenesses. Sight involves metaphysics as well as physics. A better slogan: "Being is believing."

Seeing is not merely a matter of optics. Even the matter of optics is not simply the mechanics of light. There is no sight without a seer. Sight is always a subjective process, and seeing always invokes more than the optical delineation of objective reality via the physical registration of light. Seeing propounds images, and images will jog any and all the senses—individually and in limitless combination. The poet knows this. The artist has always known this. It is this knowledge that instructs and impels the artist.

In painting, so-called op art is the old game of optical illusion given new status. Op art plays with the physics of light and color together with the mechanics of human optical perception. At the same time, it involves the metaphysics of human "seeing," that is, the capacity of the mind to entertain at least two contradictory perceptions at the same time.

This type of painting is without reference to anything but itself and the strange properties of both the human eye that sees it and the human mind that "makes it work." Such art is not tied to analogy, as is the traditional painting that represents something else, whether a portrait, still life, landscape, or whatever—even if it is an abstraction. This is beyond even the method of symbol in which the process of representation is still the motive and the goal. Instead, the *meaning* of this kind of painting is discovered exclusively in the human act of perceiving its active duplicity. Seemingly a simple, uncomplicated, emotionless form of art, the op painting develops in the viewer, as he or she studies it, an unexpected degree of not only absorption but *complicity*.

When the viewer begins to see it in a new way, in a way that "contradicts" the pattern first discerned and identified, surely a metaphorical experience of some kind is occurring. Indeed, such a painting achieves a kind of pure, even *scientific*, metaphor rather than an instructive analogy or representation of some sort because it is what it does. Furthermore, it is what *we* do when we *see* it.

Actually, there is nothing new or startling about op art unless one is anxious to keep the experience of art free of imaginative involvement and entertainment. It is a metaphorical version of the game of analogies we have all played, finding forms in nature that suddenly look like something else: the Great Stone Face, for instance, on that New England mountain—the sight of which involves more art experience than, say, the Mount Rushmore Memorial. Blink, and the Great Stone Face may again be seen simply as a granite outcropping. What we see at Mount Rushmore is a marvelous feat of engineering rather than art. To visualize the mountain as it *was* would now take the imagination of an artist. But we've all played the game with natural objects, suddenly seeing in a tree, a rock, or a cloud the shape of an animal or other object. Our national parks and scenic areas are full of institutional examples: Devil's Tower, Organ Pipe Cactus, Capitol Reef, Montezuma's Castle, Craters of the Moon, Bridal Veil Falls, and so on. Anyone who has toured a limestone cave knows the routine. The guide flashes light on a formation at the rear of the grotto: "Here we have Cleopatra's shawl, and if you step down here and look again, you have two strips of bacon, well done (murmurs of assent and delight from the crowd). And right over there we see the devil's toothbrush . . ."

I belong to this place more and more. I know this because I simply don't think about it as much. Habits take over. Routines. Grooves. I probably don't *see* as much of the cabin, the woods, as I did at first, because I know they're there. As they become more familiar, they become more subjectively a part of me, just as I perhaps become more objectively a part of the scene. Less drama? Less risk? On the way to peace. On the way to boredom?

In any event, the more I grow accustomed to this Clam Lake setting and fit into it, the more my mind moves out from it into the contrasting complexities of other places, other times, other scenes, other lives. Sometimes as I read or write, I come back with a sudden shock of displacement to the isolation of this room and myself in it. At such times I am likely to look sharply for a moment at the log walls, at the looming stone chimney, at the rigid trunks of trees beyond the big window. It is not me so much as my restless mind that seeks some less-restricted, less-finite world.

Yesterday I walked over a fresh layer of snow out to the woodpile for a supply of logs. When I returned, I was careful to place my shoes in the same stepprints I had made going out. From the cabin I was pleased looking back over the neat shoeprints that repeated my course like a gigantic dotted line.

This morning, looking out, I see the prints of a small animal beside mine. In the night he must have followed my course to investigate the possibilities in the newly uncovered logs on the woodpile. Or did he walk right along beside me yesterday?

85

Mind-extending drugs, such as LSD, may be seen as a physical (that is, chemical) means of upsetting the customary balance in the human psyche between the methods of analogy and metaphor, in overwhelming favor of the latter.

This suggests that the relationship of the psychedelic experience induced by drugs to the aesthetic experience available through the arts may be close and instructive. But analogous as the two may be, they are not the same. The difference is as much in kind as it is in degree.

In the aesthetic experience of art there is always an object—something *other*—from which the person undergoing the experience maintains a degree of separation. Even a piece of music being heard or a poem being read is in this respect an art *object*.

But in the psychedelic experience, there is no art object, there is just the experience. This is the equivalent of saying that for the person "taking the trip" the world of analogy has dissolved, and all is experienced as metaphor of one kind or another. In the collapse of normal duality as the proper ground for metaphor, the person (that is, his or her perception) becomes the art *object*. The trouble with this is that the psychedelic state allows no such divisive objectivity. This accounts for the singularity of the experience and the illogicality the person encounters later in trying to describe it or reproduce it for others. The problem is finding satisfactory grounds for analogy. There may be none.

Memory is an important key to the basic human reliance on metaphor. The reality of the past is manifest *objectively* in cause-and-effect occurrences: There are ashes in the fireplace today because I burned logs there last night. But the reality of the past is manifest *subjectively* in the mental process of memory: I recall lighting the fire, watching it roar, and getting drowsy from its heat. In both ways, however, the past informs the present, for the only sense of reality that will continue to support human life as we know it is the reality that includes past reality as an integrated part of present reality.

People close to me have died. Friends my own age. Born as I was born, with whole lives to live, like my own. Then stopped somewhere—some*when*—"back there." Rex, from my high-school days. Casual and sly, he came back from flying airplanes in the war and, in a confusion of motives on Air Force Day, with the celebrating "peacetime" bombers soaring in formation overhead, descended to his basement and hanged himself. And Hugh. Good-hearted Hugh taught everyone better than they knew from his own generous store of love, enthusiasm, humor, and reason. His heart and circulation stopped so unreasonably one strange night. Dead—years now. But they persist, still my friends—as they were, as I am—as they no doubt persist in the continuing lives of many others. In my thoughts, in my dreams, in my makeup. I know them so well—perhaps even better—for their having died so soon, so unseasonably—back there.

The human personality is made of such self-contained contradictions as are inherent in the action of memory. In memory, what is irretrievably past in fact is made present in mind. The function of memory itself, then, can be viewed as metaphorical. It imposes on the present moment a past reality that is no longer real since the past is "absolute," is without dynamics or the potential for change, and thus can have no vital reality. Yet every experience in the past has become a kind of absolute factor contributing to what we experience in the present as *truth*. There is the superimposition of opposites on each other here. The past, which is "dead," and the present, which is "alive," can, through the medium of memory, be experienced by the human as a simultaneity—just as the factors in any functioning metaphor can be yoked "unrealistically" together. The result is an understanding, rather than simply isolated experience or knowledge. The result also leads cumulatively to what we experience as the individual personality—the identity of which has continuity despite the impact of constant alteration.

Blizzard conditions when I awoke this morning. A total wraparound, mean, here-to-stay kind of storm. And me, thanks to late ruminating last night, facing a cold hearth and a low supply of firewood beside it. The first order of business this day—after I decided that despite the pervasive gloom it *was* day—was clear, and I bundled up to brave the relentless, driving snow and wind.

As I struggled over the familiar distance to the woodpile, fierce antagonistic gusts whipped raw against the exposed skin of my face, stinging my eyes so that I had to narrow them to watery slits. I moved through the heavy drifts underfoot and the thick, angry air above, hardly able to see the woodpile until I stumbled on it, directed only by habitual movements and remembered relationships of from here to there.

The return to the cabin, loaded and unbalanced arms heaped with logs, was even more treacherous, more disorienting. My movements seemed only to keep me in place amid the swirling vortices of wind and punishing snow. I breathed with increasing difficulty both from the physical effort of moving in that tumult and from what seemed an alarmingly diminished supply of air displaced by thickening snow. Even the light of day seemed threatened, and the chance of shapes or forms defining themselves in my fitful vision grew even less likely in the enveloping dark gray through which I moved. Directions—or my sense of them—whirled with the opaque air, and my wits struggled along with my legs to hold their bearings as I pitched now this way, now that, through the maelstrom. Even up and down seemed unsure in the turbulence. In a world robbed of horizon, the snow attacked as ferociously from below as from beside, ahead, and above. I lost the distinction between the snow I was walking on and the snow I was pushing through, and for a few stupefying mechanical moments I was certain that while I plunged unsteadily forward, my passage left no tracks, no visible mark behind.

When the cabin suddenly broke through—a gray-black wall of logs floating queerly through a tumbling blue-gray universe, little more than an arm's length in front of me—I awoke as if from a trance, from a vague malignant dream, my sight regained, my gyroscope reset, my sense of a past and a negotiable future restored. Leaning my shoulder against the wall, I edged my way along it to the door, found the knob with one frantic, numb, groping gloved hand, its arm still clenched stubbornly around my load of firewood, and let myself in. With an immense wave of relief, I dropped the wood immediately into the cabin and leaned back hard to slam the door against the howling malevolence of the storm. It was a bad trip.

Tonight as I sit staring entranced into the wild, roaring red-orange-yellow-blue inferno of the fireplace, the only motion anywhere is the leaping flames and, over my shoulder, the mimicking shadows they throw on the inert, cold log walls.

Were the ancients somehow aware that the dance of molecules was infinitely more rapid and frantic in hell than in heaven? Their imagery would suggest so. The faster the movement, the greater the friction, the greater the heat, and the greater the hellishness. The ideal of Hell is total friction. Would this be anything like total stimulation?

But then there was Dante, who placed the vilest sinners—and Satan himself—in the lowest circle of hell, where they were arrested in solid ice and the suspended animation of an absolute zero.

Day again, and the new snow has settled in enormous drifts, climbing the trunks of the larger trees and banked high against the side of the cabin. The wind is tamed to occasional wisps that dust loose scatters of snow from the branches. The sky is still overcast, but it is thin and brightening, the patient sun behind it promising to pierce the tired gray altogether in an hour or so and divide the world once again into blue and white.

In primitive times men worshiped the sun. We must do so again. As our rampant technology outstrips the supply of the earth's stored fuels, we must turn again and propitiate the fierce benevolent sun as the only direct source of life and energy. Amen.

Absorbed in the picture on the TV screen and caught up in the company of its "human" figures and sounds, I once again shift my view and see it as a compact and companionable but enormously complex mechanism devised of electrical circuits and intricate component parts—like nothing else in my Clam Lake cocoon.

Is the TV set more like me than, say, the fire in the fireplace?

In the world of electronic circuitry, analogical relationships are preset. They are programmed without regard for a strict according with time, certainly without the consideration of simultaneity in meaning. Regardless of how rapidly the computation is made by a computer, the process is still sequential. The electronic answer cannot be considered the product of metaphor. The answer, or response, is simply another datum, ready to take its place in analogical relationship with other data pertinent to some preset problem. In an Age of Circuitry, therefore, analogical problems may become almost exclusively the work of machines. Since the computer reduces the time and effort in analogical work to a minimum interval, let IBM do it. The human role becomes more clearly the metaphorical role—that for which the human mind is uniquely suited.

In previous ages the ideal of judgment has been relegated to a superbeing and to a religious faith in his omniscience, over which we mortals have little or no control. But judgment may now become transcendently our domain, our work. Now that our tools have acquired analogical intelligence, we are no longer the instrument as much as we are instrumental. The work of the computer, however rapidly performed, is consecutive. The work of a human, channeling this analogical ground more and more to the electronically guided machine, can become increasingly turned to the instantaneous.

My time here at the cabin in Clam Lake—the very time of day—has become as much an interior as an exterior reality. Curiously, the two are not at odds. If I wake in the morning and prefer the warmth of my bed to the uncertain air of the cabin outside it, I go back to sleep. What matter the minutes to or from whatever hour? It will be no less my morning when I do rise from bed and busy myself about breakfast. All temporal sense swells and contracts in relation to what I am about. In this regard the clock is an absurdly inaccurate measuring device. It only tells me *its* time. In my natural situation here, the passage of time is not that essentially impersonal, numerical one, moving indifferently and implacably onward at an unvarying pace, as if in spite of the humans whose minds thought it up and then gave it their fealty.

Instead, time here is continuous—as I think is its natural state—and not segmented. To me, hours, half-hours, and quarter-hours seem anachronistic. Time is available in easy accordance with my use of it. Regularity is imposed on my time only by the large unbroken cycle of light and dark as the sun moves in its continuous path across the skies to round out my day and in its course disappears across the lake to bring on the night.

A surprising realization: I stated that "the sun moves in its continuous path across the skies," thus causing day and night, but that isn't the way it works. Rather, that's the way *I* work. The sun doesn't move through our skies. As creatures on a planet in our solar system, *we* revolve around the sun. Besides that, our planet also rotates on its own axis, causing the steady alternation of day and night according to which side is facing the sun. It is we on Earth and not the sun by day or the moon and stars by night that are moving through "our skies." Yet it remains more natural to speak of it as I experience and sense it—still in human-centered terms.

Strange. My statement about time being my own was cast in pre-Copernican terms. After four centuries, the discovery by Copernicus that we are not at the center of the universe—this monumental discovery upon which our intricate mechanical systems and our finite quantitative measurements of time and space depend—still has not become the "common sense" of civilized, enlightened people. Apparently we must have it both ways, subjective and objective, the world of experience as well as the world of "fact." This means we continue to live primarily as natural and functional beings rather than as theoretical and conceptual factors.

And why not? What ever led us to suppose otherwise? I am aware of my error about the day being caused by the sun's movement across the sky *insofar as the Copernican system establishes the fact of the matter,* but I am not at all sure of any *finality* in the error. Copernicus can be updated (or backdated!) too. According to Einstein's view of universal operations, the choice of any fixed point—Earth, sun, North Star, or, for that matter, *me* with my feet on the ground here at Clam Lake—is purely arbitrary. We now have a universe in which all time and motion are understood to be relative, to be dealt with as constant solely in relation to a figurative abstraction: the speed of light. Einstein's universal reality allows us no "dead center."

Closer to home, my statement about the sun crossing my sky remains unaffected somehow by any argument that it is not scientifically accurate. I am satisfied with it because it conveys the human experience I wish to express more fully and more immediately than any version that would be factually correct. I even like it *better* for knowing that it is factually wrong. It gains strength thereby, for that knowledge has turned my experience—or at least my expression of it—to metaphor. It includes a kind of human echo that adds life, vitality, and dimension. It is closer to poetry and myth than it is to fact, for poetry and myth are more consistent with sentient experience across the ages of man than with disembodied knowledge. Their concern—our concern—is not with scientific fact as much as with human truth.

I am lucky. I am human. I do not have to choose finally between a pre-Copernican and a post-Copernican view, between a pre-Einsteinian and a post-Einsteinian universe, between the sensible experience of my actual life and whatever knowledge I may gain of a universe that expands beyond me only in relation to my growing concepts of it—a universe that will always be beyond me but of which I am no less an organic part.

94

How *can* I choose? I am *human*, and I am *a* human. I will continue to have it both ways and to live it both ways, for these ways are not absolute alternatives. I know of no absolutes that will hold. Conceptions of any absolutes are themselves relative, if only to other absolutes that have been, or might be, held. For me, in me, and through me, such alternatives co-exist and are complementary.

A huge soundless shadow swept past me as I headed back to the cabin this afternoon with dusk coming on. I ducked involuntarily and thus did not get a good look as it flew swiftly over my head and wove its way out of sight through the trees. It must have been an owl, like the one I heard the other night with its screech, followed by a hollow *whoooot*, a long pause, and then another *whoooot*. Small animals beware.

Distance is often not a matter of space as much as a matter of kinetics. Across the room, across the lake, across the country, across the years—all are defined by what it will take to get me there, to *change* me from here to there.

Early this morning I was awakened by a sharp report outside that sounded like a rifle shot. I got up nervously to see who could be firing a gun at such an hour and so close to the cabin, but nothing was in motion, nothing in sight. Later it happened again, and I discovered that it had nothing to do with guns or with people. Here and there in the intense, rigid cold, frozen trees were cracking in the frost.

I have no particular difficulty in dealing with the daily facts of my existence here—keeping warm against the cold, eating regularly, observing changes in the weather, in the woods, in my perceptions from day to day—but there is a difference between observing facts and being scientific. I find it hard these days to be scientific. I wonder if this isn't the result of my altered sense of time, my lack of attention to any constant measurement of time beyond the nature of my activity and consciousness.

In modern life, science has been taking the place of religions of the past largely because science is dedicated to apprehending and certifying time as ultimately external to our individual lives. This condition has been basic to all religious systems that have claimed people's faith in the past.

Science relies on systems in which the separability of data is measurable. We are scientific when we separate the segments within the flow and flux of time by the analogical method of subdivision into efficient units of measurement on the clock and the calendar. The microseconds, seconds, minutes, hours, days, weeks, months, years, decades of our lives are all built on analogies with the configurations and motions of the planets within our solar system—an isolated system of mechanics, of time and motion, which only apparently do not evolve or change.

But these systems, these notions of time, must now be regarded as conveniences, as efficient units of measurement, not as ultimate and ceaseless necessities. They are local options, so to speak. In the universal scheme of relationships being sought through our reach into the cosmos by Einsteinian and post-Einsteinian relativity, they are a species of systematized human percepts, not immutable law.

There is no cause to blame "science" or to fault the scientist for today's ills. Science has been devoted to manipulating time and memory in the insensible world, the world as things, the world in which identification is rationalized by analogy through the analysis of likenesses and differences, by classification, by defining "norms" against which to measure. This is an operation of the mind in which memory is treated as if it were substantial rather than metaphorical, in which, to put it in more topical terms, experience is admissible only as verified and separable data.

The need is not to reform science, which is doing fine, but to rehabilitate ourselves. Much of the problem resolves in the nature and process of human language, the basis of which is metaphor, the goal of which is poetry. Our language enables us to handle both fact and truth and, in a peculiarly human way, to *substantiate* our experience. It enables us to commit experience to forms that are at once ours and not ours, of our time and at least in token fashion external to our time; for as surely as the word belongs to us, we belong to the word.

In bed late last night, trying to coax sleep from the almost solid quiet and dark that seemed to reject me in utter indifference, trying to empty my tired mind and close out the last consciousness of the long day, I was instead suddenly and totally taken over by the thought of: *Anne.* For no particular reason, the gap of years separating us had closed, like thunder after a bolt of lightning, and her whole image—*she*—was there. Her eyes. Her skin. Her aura. Her grace. My innocent, inarticulate, total sense of *her*. So close after all the years lost to me. I almost melted in the immediacy and wraparound warmth of unencumbered love, more enveloping, more whole in memory than it could ever have been in reality. Then almost at once I found myself thinking, not *her*, but *about* her; and the totality of feeling dissolved. *Was* she somehow there in the night? Was it only me? Could there have been any such total *we*?

I was alone, but the dark was alive again and listening, and I knew myself alive in it.

Love is being able to see the world through the eyes of another, not just on one matter, but as if on all matters. Romantic love is bred by the universal wish for this confluence between two people. Love becomes mature when it achieves this state through understanding as well as through wishing.

Religious love is no exception. It strives to see the world and understand it as an unseen God sees it. In religions that have an intermediate human example of such total love, such as Jesus in Christianity, the goal is to love God through the love of the intermediary human model. To love Jesus is to see the world as Jesus viewed it, in the assurance that Jesus wholly saw and understood the world as you see it. Such reciprocity is the ideal, but of course this runs contrary to the facts of our individuated lives.

The basis of love, therefore, depends on the human practice of metaphor and not on analogy or mere comparison. To compare one's own life with that of another is to use analogy. This can produce a great variety of responses, such as pity, envy, superiority, or inferiority; but it cannot produce love or true compassion. To accept the terms and conditions of another life as essentially one's own demands the method of metaphor. This is structured in the nature of love.

In love we are not so much selfless as we are our best selves, literally through another, or, in the larger sense, through others. In love we are still physically bound to the objective facts of existence, but we are projected and enabled by human sympathies that give us identities well beyond our single, separate, isolated, limited lives.

Justice, it is well to remember, is an ideal and an abstraction. So, in our intellectual firmament, is love. Yet we can affirm from the testament of our own lives and from what we can gather through the testimony of others that men and women can know justice and that men and women can experience love. Wisdom in compromise with the ideal— as often as not an unconscious compromise—makes it so. And *compromise*, looked at closely, is *mutual promise*, or the shared commitment to hope and faith.

I watched the beaver house in the frozen flowage at the far end of the lake for a long while this afternoon, hoping to see some sign of beaver life, maybe even the shaggy fellows themselves, but whatever the colony was up to was all within. There was no sign of life from my vantage outside. I pictured them nudging one another in there and chewing absently on the soaked bark of the birch trees cut from their winter feed beds months ago and dragged under the water to lodge in their winter pantry at home. Could they, with their keen beaver senses, picture me watching?

How could I ever have supposed that I might run away from words? True, they do pile up—behind our eyes and our ears as well as behind our tongues. But without them we are mere integers, unable to suppose or to be supposed.

I am not as alone in this solitary winter retreat as I would have thought. Or, rather, I am not so *lonely*. I am, after all, quite alone. So are we all, but *lonely* is an attitude, a mood. I am too busy these days for that. Nevertheless, the places I've been in the past, the scenes I've seen, and the people I've known do not leave me even though for a time I have left them. My memory is clear, accessible, and active enough, and it serves. In fact, I can't get away, can't step clear of it. I must be cautious under my solitary circumstances not to overindulge it. When nostalgia comes, can loneliness be far behind?

While I am busy with my days, every day casts the long shadow of its night.

MIAMI BEACH

What green there was those days (those restless days)
Moved on the windblown surface of the sea.

The clouds conspired and altered overhead. Shadows
Followed out their course. (And so did we.)

On land, the freight of items took its count:
The whited buildings numbered, people tagged,
The streets, the rooms, the keys, the price of meals,
The registry of cash, the minutes to the hour.
Still, the land grew somehow safe—despite its paint,
Its deadly plaster, and its merely horizontal time—
Because we watched the green and saw the sea.

We saw the sea-green changes, and we felt the heavy
Wildness of the boil below. We saw the change, and yet,
For all the surface shift, the roar, the froth and foam,
Incessant action pushing in with wave on wave a-glitter
At the tips—for all of this, it was the selfsame sea
That Whitman saw, that Arnold saw, that wise Ulysses
Saw and mastered—till it mastered him.

                                        And love
Was once again the birth of Venus, seaborne,
Bringing to the tilted palms of crass hotels
Her elemental, countless circumstance that
Played, in sea-girt Florida, the best of jokes
On all the shore-bound things we knew. (We knew.)

Sea waves are not the sort of ordered things
That one adds up. Like greens that plumb
The sunlight's debt to shadow; like air we breathe;
Like all the pain and pleasure yet to come;
Like life, and death, and love (and love);
They are already (and they always are) their sum.

The concentration of poetic language and form is a matter of economy with words, but this must not be confused with mere efficiency. Rather, poetry combines the goal of technology, which is efficiency, with the goal of religion, which is sufficiency.

"Make love, not war" is an example of an efficient statement, but it will not really suffice, being better suited to advertising than to the humanistic purpose it proposes. It *mocks* poetry rather than *being* poetry. It is mechanical. Its basis is an analogy, and a false one at that. What a shallow and flat slogan it is beside W. H. Auden's parallel assertion: "We must love one another or die." That is theological substance—simply, memorably, and gracefully put. Good poetry is always theological, just as good theology is always poetic.

THE PASSIONATE GRAMMARIAN TO HIS LOVE

cop'u·la, n.; 1. That which connects, a link. 2. Also
copulative verb. *Gram.* A link verb; as, the verb *be*,
which has little meaning of its own, is sometimes
called "the copula." 3. *Logic.* The relation or
connecting link between the subject and the
predicate of a proposition.

My teeter-totter world admires a state
Of balance: the terms of time and self
Held double, coupled, each with each.

Pairs persist, dear girl, with tense released:
One is, two are—the one forever being
Now, the two continuing.

Complement me, then; intransitively be:
For odds support no singleness, and even
Up must satisfy with down.

Quod erat demonstrandum est, my dear:
All concord posits linking verbs, i.e.:
The copulae of we.

Maybe a contributing reason so many people in our age feel alien to poetry is that they are conditioned to see and to make or accept images in the comparatively cold and objective fashion of the camera. I wonder if the much-discussed lack of personal identity in our time, the other-directedness, the alienation of the individual in the midst of "the lonely crowd," and the cult of computerlike objectivity may be related to our tendency to substitute a photographed reality for the experience of the sentient human being. Might not the use of so many irrational images and sequences in contemporary literature be somehow the artist's response in words to the irreproachable rationalism and firm time-sense of the photograph? Might not the appeal of drugs, psychedelic visions, and op art be in part the promise of an escape for image-making humans from the tyranny of a realism defined by that immensely useful but insensate and dumb instrument—the camera?

The prevailing image of reality in our time may be not

so much in the eye of the beholder as it is in the lens of the camera. We are becoming so accustomed to the wholesale photographic reproduction of our world (along with past worlds, the worlds that are no more) that our very way of seeing and registering reality has been grossly affected—and altered. Since the method of language, the method of metaphor, is rooted in the image, in what we used to call without embarrassment "the mind's eye," our dependence on the photograph, which gives us an image of reality arrived at without going through the human brain, is a revolution in epistemology, in the matter of how we know what we know.

It pains me to think that this large sheet of glass that reveals to me in its succession of moods the marvelous northern Wisconsin woods may have been installed as a "picture window."

One way—a plausible way—to discriminate between the modern and premodern worlds would be to underline the tremendous impact of photography on our sense of reality in the last hundred years. The "realities" of war, for instance, start for us with the American Civil War—thanks to Matthew Brady's on-the-scene camera. Any previous war is somehow simply historical and must be imagined, that is, it must be brought to our sense of reality by way of suggested images and subjective arrangements, as in literature like Stephen Crane's *Red Badge of Courage,* or the *Iliad,* or a painting like Benjamin West's *Death of Wolfe,* or

Tschaikowsky's *1812 Overture*. For most practical purposes, we are modern in the common manner when both our public orientation to reality and our personal vision have become photographic.

My picture of the American tourist-photographer is a caricature: Cameras and equipment strap him in, like a beast of burden in harness. He spreads over the earth (wild, irrational image suddenly of the old Sherwin-Williams paint trademark) clicking and clicking away, rarely seeing anything directly and wholly for himself, but forever asking his camera to do the seeing.

And then, for the rest of his life, his recollection of his experiences will persist chiefly in the collection of images on the film he exposed. Indeed, memory in the life of the individual (and memory writ large is history) becomes pinpointed and congested, so to speak, in sequences of photographs, each one a minor epiphany.

Why should I feel so ambivalent about photography? Because I want to protect my *wordiness*? Since the photograph is not the thing it represents, its function is clearly figurative. The question is not whether the photograph is a lie or not. Of course it is. The question is whether we view it through the method of analogy or metaphor.

The camera stops actuality in its tracks; then the photograph gives us a reconsidered perception of it. Even in "moving" pictures, it is the human viewers and not the photographs that provide the motion. Animals, looking at photographs, do not recognize (re-cognize!) the other reality represented in the photographic images. Apparently they see only the present materiality before them. Looking at a television picture, the family dog or cat apparently sees only what to us is the television *set*, but we humans see with unconscious duplicity. We not only see the images, the figures; we also accept them unquestioningly as real. Allowing only for temporal discrepancy—something our figurative minds do with ease—we accept them as identical with the actual life they represent.

We can be rational and logical about it too, treating the photograph and discussing it when we wish, merely as itself—a device, a technique or its result, a replication that takes liberty with size and space, dimension and corporeality, as well as with time. But we have it both ways with the photograph: We just as easily—maybe more easily—set aside such technicalities and invest our assent in the validity of its imagery. We not only believe what it stands for, we believe what it is. In a technological age, this is an act of metaphorical faith—perhaps the most typical and widespread one of our time.

Aside from those closed off in books and magazines, this cabin has no photographs. At least none that I've found. Extraordinary. No family portraits or snapshots. No catatonic moments embalmed in silver nitrate. *Fixed* might be a better verb—both in the sense of the neutralizing solution or "fixer" and the inability to regenerate, having been operated on. No graven images here, at any rate.

Nevertheless, the camera in its own way, extends our grasp in many directions. The photograph, however frozen and unmanageable, is a means of certifying the past to the present—more focused and indifferent than memory. Even while it denies or at best counterfeits life and movement, it has its usefulness and validity in our lives—like the concept of a static moment in time.

The telescope and microscope have so far transcended the limitations of human physiology that they require a camera, a sophisticated mechanism, and a photographic plate in order to register—ultimately for our sight and comprehension—those macrocosmic and microcosmic representations of reality that lie beyond and below us but which we can believe through their photographic images to be valid representations.

The camera even defeats time in providing us images of the "real" universe, for the camera can stop action and allow us to study the dynamics of nature as if its truths were static. The age-old explosion of the stars and the incredibly swift movement of subatomic particles in the physicist's bubble chamber are alike rendered visible—and therefore "real" to us—on the sensitized plates of the laboratory camera. In addition, we can see time and motion out of joint (in a fashion that Shakespeare could manage only with language) in the slow-motion and fast-motion movie. We can collapse hours, days, or months of deliberate growth or change into the capsule movement of time-lapse photography.

We accept the fact that these wonders are taking liberties with reality. There is much of the method of metaphor in their techniques and in our techniques when we view and accept their images.

Cameras are giving us our first images of the "realities" of space—the far side of the moon, for instance, which until recently only a cow had seen, just before the dish ran away with the spoon.

I wonder if anything in this century has had more significant effect on the perspectives from which we see ourselves than the remarkable color photographs of our planet taken by spacecraft from a great enough distance to see us whole. There it is (there we are)—the blue planet Earth, recorded objectively by the indifferent lens of a camera. Our whole self-contained ecosphere has been photographed from the outside. Now we can believe in it as irrefutable fact, for the camera has recorded it.

Another common response to the whole new image of our world as photographed from space beyond our atmosphere—a world in which we can now see all individual life subsumed—is the one that poets and naturalists have already recorded in *their* way: Our planet Earth is beautiful.

So far, the history of literature—or, better yet, the history *in* literature—is the best record we have of the shifting, developing concepts and images of reality. But the lumpy approach of the anthologies of literature that I consult in this cabin puts all writers in the same plane, regardless of when they wrote. All in the same type face. The horizons never seem to change. The landscape apparently is always the same; only the style of rendering it in words changes from age to age.

Historians of science know better. The world view and ideas of reality change often enough in *their* recounting of the past. Odd that when we marshal our literary past we should be so disinclined to follow the shifts in civilized orientation to reality. This would seem the obvious way to order the humanities, but we have virtually given it over to the sciences. As a result, we have a clear enough record of *what* people were thinking at various stages of Western culture, but our awareness of *how* they thought about what they thought is generally neglected.

In every age, the metaphorical imperative demands that people fasten on a scheme of reality within which their analogy-making activities can continue to function reasonably. Needless to say, the image-making reality of each succeeding era then becomes *the* valid one; yet the continuity and oneness of human experience is such that the literature and artistic expression of every age maintains its value and its accessibility to human truth for us, regardless of the prevailing image the artist's imagination followed.

We cannot expect our age to be an exception. The difficulty comes in trying to recognize from inside our own system of reality, the image-making apparatus through which we accept it and give it our sense of order and belief. Hindsight is easier. I can see that the medieval mind depended on an allegorical reality in which the physical world disguised spiritual truths. I can understand the Renaissance world as ana-logical reality. And the so-called Age of Reason as Isaac Newton assumed it—a universe working in the image of a machine. Very well, but what of our orientation?

I wonder if it isn't the photograph—both the still and the motion picture—that gives us our prevailing image of reality today. "Do you get the picture?" we ask one another when we want to know if we are understood. Maybe we should ask, "Does the picture get us?" Although it is difficult to face the matter squarely, it is probable that, as a people, we have more faith in the actual reality of the image in the photograph than we do in the transitory image registered directly by our own eyes—and most certainly than we do in the image rendered by the word on the page, by the poet in the poem.

There is no assurance that the role of literature in our lives will continue to be what it has been in the past. It is not unlikely, as a matter of fact, that a part of its image-making role has already been taken over by photography, rather as Christianity once took over the role previously filled by ancient myth and superstition.

In consequence, all literature will probably become more and more poetic, in the broad sense of that term, and less and less a structured accounting of events. This latter function will be taken over by the social sciences, which share the documentary approach with the photograph.

The value of literature, however, will not decrease; it will be displaced. If this is true, literature will be read and regarded more and more for its humanizing potential and less and less for its informative features. Literary experience will not then be so easily mistaken for actual experience, as has too often—and sometimes disastrously—been true in the past.

I am reading too great a variety of books while living too little a variety of life—a much less-satisfactory imbalance than the other way around.

Set against the geology of this Clam Lake area, with its rolling glacial ridges and craterlike depressions, its granite boulders and outcroppings, how short a time separates my steps through the covering woods from the steps of the American Indians here before me. How much more a part of this scene were they in their time than I in mine?

January: the month of Janus.
Janus: n. (L), *in Roman mythology*, the god who was guardian of portals and patron of beginnings and endings; he is shown as having two faces, one in front, the other at the back of his head, symbolizing his powers.

The best mirrors are the ones you can see through—like the window here at night, with the light of the room behind me and the dark snow-forest scene outside serving as backing to the glass. My reflection and that of the whole room is clear and detailed, but so is the cold, still scene outside into which these images are projected, on which we—the warmly lit room and I—are superimposed.

A curious thing about the search for identity. The answer to the question, Who am I? is that you are always at least two persons (and more probably a minimum of three) and that the degree of integration in this multiplicity of self determines the integration of character. It is character we seek in the pursuit of our identity.

At the first level of duality we are at the same time subjects and objects. We are, first of all, the persons we suppose ourselves to be from the primary but restrictive viewpoint of self. This is the subjective *I*, which can objectif itself only through assuming the rhetorical posture made possible by the grammatical concept of *me*. At the same time, we are *him* or *her*. We are, to any other person, another. We have a separate, exterior, and objectlike being, an identity as fact, you might say, rather than as truth. ("Ah, to see ourselves as others see us," we say. At the same time we seek always to be really understood by others on our own terms, to have others see us as we see ourselves.)

Everyone lives in the matrix of this inner and outer selfhood. Whoever brings the two into focus, whoever achieves a metaphorical unity of these two facets of personality without insisting on the disappearance of one in the other, is a person of character, a person who is achieving his or her identity.

The process of personal integration, however, is immensely complex, for we are engaged in our lives and in the lives of others as complex rather than simple personalities. A man can be identified simultaneously as son, father, brother, friend, enemy, husband, lover, employer, employee, colleague, rival, and so on. For each of these roles as seen by others, we have an answering sense of self-identification, and we act accordingly; yet we need to persist throughout our lives in the basic notion of the continuity of the self. Identity depends also on some fundamental sameness, some metaphysical personal ground common to all the moments we live and all the roles we fill. In this respect we may be identified in terms of a third sense of self or, to use a term that echoes the spiritual center of all religions, a third *person* or a "ground of Being."

We can become ecstatically aware of this when integration occurs suddenly through a selfhood that is whole by virtue of being at once inner and outer. We call such integration a mystical experience, one that cannot be parsed, that is beyond conventional analogy. It is an experience that approximates pure metaphor—wordless and timeless—in which one is both lost and found as a self.

On a less dramatic and more everyday plane, such awareness is something that all human lives and all living persons, past and present, may share. It is an identity-at-large that transcends selfhood by itself as either the subject or the object of living. It is implicit in the metaphorical imperative, the human method that forever grants us ourselves in the assured continuity of our lives and yet withholds in the unfulfilled process of time our truest identity.

What I write out in a fury of rapt conjecture in the incandescent core of the night often turns out to have a tame and rather hollow ring in the light of day; yet the persistent ghost of its excitement remains. Something was there in the night, and I knew it. I held it for a moment and turned it, but the next morning the light is merciless outside, and the flame burns low within. I have a bleary eye, a stubble of beard, and a pronounced difficulty in determining what all the *it's* in my illuminated manuscript referred to on the glorious night before. (Sing to the tune of "Eine kleine Nachtmusik Goes a Long, Long Way" or "The Night Has a Thousand Ayes.")

A new set of tracks just outside the cabin this morning, fresh and clearly printed in the lightly crusted snow, small doglike prints leading right up to the window, where they made a confusion of marks before returning at an angle into the woods.

That authenticates the high, sharp barking I thought I heard off a way from the cabin last night after I'd made my late cup of coffee and returned to my writing at the table—barks that I began to doubt I'd actually heard when in the ensuing stillness, despite my focused listening, there was no further sound. Fox. And he had come up to investigate the cabin. He had been right there on the drifted snow that put him up at the level of the window, studying the creature inside, no doubt—watching me at the table as I wrote, oblivious myself to anything but my words and their tracks across my brain, across the page, oblivious in the pride of my own pursuit of self to anything as immediate and quick as a fox in the snow, ranging far since the storm for his partridge or rabbit and drawn to the cabin by the curious smells and the curious yellow light thrown out onto his familiar Clam Lake snowscape and that curious figure at the table. A fox, studying me with fox curiosity, fox hunger, fox eyes, as I, no less rapt, studied myself.

Was he still in the neighborhood? Would he be back? Could I somehow see him and reverse the situation? Introduce myself, beg indulgence, and hold silent conversation? I bundled up, laced on the snowshoes, and took off after the tracks that had taken him back into the woods.

They led me in a wide semicircle to the west of the cabin and back in to the side of the porch, then away again and down the southwest slope to the lake. There they followed the shoreline for perhaps a quarter-mile, a straight line of march—or of fox trot—along the edge of the open expanse of smooth, windswept snow that covered the thick ice of the lake. The line of shrubs and trees that marked the hidden shoreline undulated in irregular scallops a short distance to our left.

When the tracks veered suddenly to the right and struck out across the lake, I followed dutifully for another quarter-mile, out in the open, feeling strangely exposed and ponderous in my mountain of man-clothes, puffing spurts of condensed man-breath into the Clam Lake air, adding the enormous clublike prints of my clumsy snowshoes to the clean, almost dainty tracks of the fox in the otherwise unmarked snow-surface of the lake.

When we got to the other shoreline, the fox continued straight into the brush, on to the waiting barren trees, up the slight slope and beyond, into the frozen anonymity of the northern Wisconsin winter woods.

I stopped and, pulling my fingers out of their separate compartments in the heavy knit linings of my leather gloves, curled them and their numbness into the comparative warmth of fists. I looked back over my shoulder across the half-mile expanse of open snow at the distant suggestion of the cabin—small, dark, diminished, mostly hidden by the tree trunks staggered between it and the lake. I made the elaborate turn required by the snowshoes and headed back in as direct a path as possible toward hearth and home.

A man living without a woman is like a sailboat under full sail but moving only in response to such wind as the sailor can blow with his own breath. The same figure works for existentialists.

What a curiously womblike situation I am in here, snug and solitary within the protecting walls of the cabin, provided with the warmth and nourishment my body needs for my mind and nervous system to develop, for my lambent thought to form.

A person must be a working part of something that is developing, of something that is going on. I am inclined to believe in this regard that every person carries clandestinely within his or her psychological being a personal recollection of his or her own preexistence, by which I mean one's own embryonic stage, one's own perfect becoming.

It may well be, as Carl Jung tells us, that contained within such a recollection is a collective unconscious—the inchoate recapitulation of all the reiterated patterns of thought and modes of growth that preceded the individual's own human birth and that help to compose each person's peculiar identity by establishing first the ground of his or her being, a background for growth, and a total human makeup to the present.

Man is born of woman and must therefore refer to her perpetually. Paradoxically, the only time he is free of this need is when he is physically a part of woman—when he is forming in the womb of his mother, wholly in the process of becoming, when his whole being is a part of and continuous with the currents and recapitulations of organic life in her being. At birth he is physically cut free, but his psychological freedom at that same instant moves into bondage. He must return to woman (or her surrogate), first as a child, with a child's need to be fostered, and then as a man, to join with woman, himself to foster others as he may.

That preexperience in the womb, that inexorable growth-and-becoming, is never possible to retain after birth, only to approximate, to imitate, to recollect, and to seek by both psychological and physiological means.

Any religious or philosophical view that calls on a state analogous to the forming-in-the-womb is an accommodation to this recollection-and-search. Furthermore, if a religious or philosophical system features both the inevitability of individual growth toward independence and the ideal of dependence upon the "parent" factors that grant growth its total potential, then it duplicates the condition of the womb and the embryonic human being developing within it.

In the Western world, ideas of heaven have drawn on such parallels, reaching back psychically into a sense of bliss in which conflict is erased and identity is vaguely assured but lacks the stain of mortality that comes with individual, separate existence. Heaven in the West usually depends on this kind of preconception. Dante's Paradiso, for instance, has this sort of pure being to distinguish it from the other realms of his universe. Wordsworth, in his "Ode: Intimations of Immortality," reflects the same conjectural sense of the paradisiacal state. The Mormons teach the preexistence of the individual soul before birth, pictured curiously in the identifiable form and shape of the mortal it will become on earth. What is most conventionally conceived of in Western culture as the realm of "pure spirit," as in a Christian heaven, may take its credibility from a prebirth recollection, which was in actuality "pure body."

In the Orient, the process of achieving a pure state of being has been more clearly one of traveling back into the earlier stages of becoming. The Eastern mystic is likely to equate pure being with a perfectly bodiless condition—indeed with a state of nonbeing. If one can attune oneself to a state analogous with the embryonic, he or she can achieve at least a stasis of the mind and of the conscious burden of self. Beyond this, if one can deny his or her physical being and negate all the features incumbent upon the individual human at birth (including those growth features at work in the womb that got under way in the first place through the play of human desire), one may approximate a state that is no state—a pure negation that reaches back beyond creation itself for its analogy, that becomes pure metaphor in the equation of opposites and therefore totally preexistent. This is union with the godhood that precedes any God. It would be much closer to Mother Earth, I should think, than to God the Father.

Next question: How does a woman achieve *her* identity? When she develops *as a woman*, are there distinctively female patterns? Is there such a thing as a human being, or are there only men and women? The concept of *a human* is exceedingly metaphorical. The Women's Liberation leaders are demanding that we all believe and act on that metaphor.

Consider the astronaut's photograph looking "down" at our blue planet Earth. Our blue color is striking and something of a surprise. From here at Clam Lake—from anywhere I might stand on this globe—when I look *up*, it is the *sky* that is blue. Heaven and Earth . . . it all depends on your angle of vision.

The concern with death that so much occupies our lives, the need to fight it somehow and put off its inevitability, is a displacement of our best intention. Perhaps the frontier, the barrier in our understanding, lies behind us, so to speak, rather than ahead. It is not "life after death" so much as "condition before birth" that holds human destiny, that best directs our investigation, inspires our deepest conjecture, and formulates our basic metaphors of hope.

Character is determined by what one respects; the rest is personality or style.

Style is a matter of how you *handle* things. It is movement, touch, arrangement, speed, care, and carelessness, not just how you handle words, but how you pick up a child, pet a dog, or make and throw a snowball.

The Oriental approach to life is based on a pervading sense of its *transcience;* the approach characteristic of Western civilization is based on a sense of *change*. One is a static interlude between states; the other, between progressive stages.

I have been here alone long enough now to assume a sameness in the days. I have developed routines. I am less and less stimulated by the observation of my surroundings, and I find myself turning my observations more and more inward. I still wonder if my season here will lead to any real change after I leave, or if it will be merely a novel interruption—an interlude on a solitary stage.

Maintenance, I might do well to keep in mind, has always been important to the West, not to the East.

It is cold these days, these nights. Must I devise a false ceiling in this cabin to keep the warmth down here where I live?

I suppose that only humans count to more than *two*. *Two*, it would seem, is the extent of clear differentiation among other animals. Beyond *two* is a more general diversity, but diversity is still *two*-ness, plus a matter of proportion, of volume, of frequency: many. It is all binary at base. Beyond *two* is confusion—at best, the problematical.

Animals do not think of themselves; they think *for* themselves.

I wonder if the concept of *one* isn't the most unlikely of all numbering. It is probably a uniquely human device: the thinker separated conceptually from the thought—from *I* to *me*. *Me* has no credence without the possibility of another who, given subjectivity identical to mine, can also think of

120

himself as *me*. Seen this way, *me* becomes the basis of all that we consider humane thought. And the extension of our personal pronouns from *he—she—me* to the suprapersonal *one* is a highly metaphysical act. Only humans can count to *less* than two.

All knowledge and all expression that conveys it proceeds on the principle of likeness and difference. The forms of classification that give objective order to scientific knowledge are structured on the basis of similarities and differences, but I suddenly see that all human sense of order depends first of all on our ability to know similarity—sameness. Without the sense of sameness present in some degree, we could have no sense of order. Complete and total difference—a world in which there is no sense of sameness—would be a world of total chaos.

Fortunately, each passing instant is not anarchic, and the world is not chaos to those who live in it. It would be chaos were it not for our recognition of likenesses—and therefrom of unlikenesses. And the likeness that makes order—even the search for order—essential for us is the likeness of all living things—past, present, and future—in their inevitable common fate: each to its own death.

Seen from another angle, likeness is the basic form of affirmation. Unlikeness (and thus any form of negation) follows in our conceptualization of alternatives as the necessary complement of likeness, which remains primary for us.

From this necessary sequence that we bring to bear on the way leading from primal chaos to ultimate order (both of which are, for us, imagined states), we derive the primacy of hope over indifference or despair. We are born to hope. The human brain we inherit has hope structured in as an essential method. "Cross my heart" we used to say as children when we most needed to be believed, "and hope to die."

One more try at analogy and metaphor. I'm not sure I have them yet.

The analogy (like its miniature, the simile) leads the imagination by an honest path of open, reasonable comparison, that is, it holds the things being compared in their places while we size them up in relation to each other.

The metaphor, on the other hand, is unreasonable. It is a "deliberate lie" that contains its truth not *as* a solution but *in* solution. It demands that we dissemble even as we assemble, that we pursue unity through a willing duplicity with "the facts." Thus it defies the world of fact, but while fact may be simple (fact *aims* to be simple), truth is always complex. Fact must seek its rational place in an ordered universe. Truth need not be rational. In fact, the highest truths often defy the order below them. They are notoriously irrational.

The analogy, then, holds apart, and the metaphor puts together. The analogy illustrates; the metaphor illuminates. Through analogy we can certify continuation; through metaphor we can know continuum.

Children respond to rhythm before they can recognize fact. Maybe the one makes the other possible.

CHILD'S PLAY

Today the way trees tossed reminded me
of half-forgotten sorceries that stitch
such instants in a seamless colloquy:

A child I knew and watched, bewitched
by repetition as he played alone,
would chant, "Again? . . . O.K."—as if he wished

to stay the moment he had come to own
and reproduce its sure effect again
as cause. The thing he'd done in play had grown

to simple truth. In action, truth had been
the fact of doing and the act of something known.
He did again his antic motion, and the reign

of pleasure measured on. Each time he won
the game. "Again? . . . O.K." The mimicry
once more connected arts of calling forth

with sciences of truth. But then, my tree?
Well, who can measure such an antic motion's worth
as trees responding to the wind's fiat?

It's just that somehow I believe I know
the countless times the trees have tossed like that
in play; and every time, "again? . . . o.k."—and Oh!

God has generally been posited in systematic theology by way of analogy, a means of teaching, but the way to know God has always been by way of metaphor, a means of experiencing. The concept of God is notoriously difficult to discuss and accept in conventional, rational prose. It should be since it rests in the essential irrational metaphor at the root of all creation. It deals in an essential paradox for the human mind: *the lie we can believe.* It calls on the same process our minds employ in metaphor—considering diverse elements, not separately, but together, simultaneously, and thus *both out of time and as if for all time.* It is the method of attaining within the mind's intensive reality a revelation that cannot be wholly rational or externalized, a personal realization of the unity in diversity. Such poetic insight is an experience that is not so much an advance in knowledge or conception as in thought and perception.

Why should I be so concerned with ideas of God lately? I have no church, no stake in any particular deity. Do I really care, I wonder, or is it just extended curiosity, a kind of ultimate intellectual gamesmanship? After all, there's no one around to contend with my speculations—except maybe the red squirrel who just now punctuated my thought by scampering noisily along the edge of the eaves where the snow has blown free. Or the occasional croaking ravens and their cousins, the scolding jays (who I am increasingly sure are passing comments about *me*). The rest is pretty much silence. Immense silence, over and around the sounds I make (sounds that only I and my kind can believe have any significance beyond themselves).

Maybe such a combination answers my questions: the human's creaturehood and self-consciousness (tending toward paranoia); the human's fate and hope (tending toward faith); God's silence.

Throughout recorded history, the concept of deity has functioned as a counterpart or complement to human limitations within the most basic metaphors we could employ to underwrite the continuity of human existence. God is the complement of human beings, therefore, because God is the image—or, better yet, the *reflexion*—of human hope, of humankind's possibly limitless, yet always limited, potential for growth. As long as we are unfulfilled, we will need an identifiable deity; and as long as we maintain an identifiable deity, we will remain unfulfilled.

This is another paradox that can seem self-canceling. If, however, we can reduce such a paradox to metaphor, we find we can accept such a self-contradictory idea as is expressed in the phrase "the eternal now."

The God-concept, then, is our means of supposing continuous mental identities even though the inexorable passage of physical time apparently (or rationally) precludes them. This is why the world of fact, the world of scientifically ascertainable phenomena, is just as much an essential "lie" as is the essential metaphor. We must act as if every fact exists for all time when, as a part of the evolutionary whole, it is perpetually subject to change—if only in its relativity to other facts. Facts have their significance only in relation to other facts.

Deity is our complement in the symbolic need to relate

all seemingly unresolvable clashes that only time—when it is viewed simultaneously as human time and God's time, as now and forever—could actually resolve. The God-man metaphor is the way in which we simultaneously contain and relate essential opposites: being with nonbeing, matter with spirit, time with eternity.

The evolutionary sense of eternity, in turn, conceives this as a perpetually growing relationship. Old metaphors—or at any rate the old terms of any metaphor—can wear out and lose their ability to absorb and reflect growth for us. It is our language that most overtly directs and demonstrates how metaphor works and what metaphor therefore *is*, but language itself is subject to change, growth, and evolutionary metamorphosis. In a radically new age, radically new metaphors are needed to deal contemporaneously with the nature of the relationship between the individual and his or her hope—that is, between humankind's growing knowledge and evolving way of knowing: between the complementary factors of the essential metaphor.

I am startled by the thought that historical humanity is on the brink of birth, of assuming actual, rather than potential, responsibility for human life—for all life as we know it. Yet there is much to make that thought worth playing with. What we know of the patterns of life on the biological scale together with what we are learning on the anthropological and theological scales (these being, in the fullest sense possible to us at this time, the *historical* scale) strongly suggest as a kind of metaphor that humanity is concluding that period of gestation throughout which it has considered itself a part of a parent being—even biologically attached to that parent if one chooses to see the mythologies of Christ and other god-identified mortals in the world's religions in that light.

In this figure, we are about to emerge into a world, not of our own making, but of our own, a world in which we may draw breath and assume a separate sense of existence, yet a world in which we may learn new sets of essential relationships (or new ways of experiencing essential relationships) through metaphor as well as through analogy. It will be a world in which one must become conscious of one's own existence, not only as biologically human (that would be a kind of perpetuated embryonic stage), but as fully historic, separate, responsibly human.

In the "God Is Dead" theologies we have begun to see the terms of the essential metaphor change, but God is dead only as humankind becomes truly alive. The metaphorical relationship that contains, opposes, and unites both God and humanity will have to adapt. The terms of our essential metaphor will evolve. God is dead in order that hope may not die.

When one is cut, there is a vital need to bleed. There is something unnerving and distinctly unfair, therefore, about a paper cut. It hurts and continues to hurt sharply, but that is all. No blood. It's almost as if the hurt is borrowed and the pain is abstract, not rightly yours. Without the natural flow of blood to wash, draw, and close the wound, the paper cut is notoriously hard to heal.

I've had this one on my right forefinger for days now, and it continues to smart and burn under any pressure. Since it runs parallel with the ridges of my fingerprint, it is hard to see as well as hard to heal. It often reminds me that I was careless some time back in dealing with the sharp edge on a simple piece of paper. Ludicrous, when I stop to consider it—suffering and carrying on about a paper cut here in this isolated cabin, in these indifferent Clam Lake woods. To extend the irony, if not the humor, it is just possible that the paper responsible for it had its source in pulpwood cut from this very forest. And me here now, cut to the quick and hurting in this embarrassing unseen fashion—clean, dry, and bloodless.

Odd that the least grievous type of indigestion should be called "heartburn."

The halls of thought, no matter how tall and stately, are apt to be drafty.

Most words whistle.

I recall with amusement a spirited conversation held some years ago with a close friend, one with whom I felt at the time an exceptional rapport. It concerned the aesthetic effect of toilet paper installed to unroll over the top, as against that which unrolls—more discreetly, I suppose—from behind and below, like a comma. We agreed that it was infinitely preferable to have the paper unroll from underneath. The elation in our total agreement seemed, I recall, profound, as if we had somehow notched another advance in the human search for cosmic order.

There are times, I must record, when the books that line the shelves around this cabin become an encumbrance, almost a mute judgment, upon me. So many minds. So many books. The ages, the ages . . . So much life and thought committed to the order of pages and print, and none of it—not even the total of it—any more than a ghostly echo to this quick edge of the living moment I inhabit. There they stand shoulder to shoulder, stiff between their covers, in almost military ranks on the shelves that surround me. At times, books are not company. They are *a* company.

Am I really doing anything these days? I largely ignore the place, the shifts of weather, the snow-still woods, and the hidden life in it. I seldom go out except to cut and split wood, then haul it in and burn it. I fix simple, unimaginative food and eat it without savor or attention while flipping pages of a book or staring absently into the fire. True, I read at times with more concentration than ever before. Occasionally I push my speculation, writing under a kind of quiet compulsion, into new and curious corners. The more I move into abstract conjecture, though, the less I am concerned with what pleased me most when I first arrived— the length of time in which to *see* the things I look at around me, the reinstatement of the things of the natural world and my practical place among them.

Am I occupied or merely preoccupied? Am I any closer to knowing what I came for, or am I somehow losing ground?

How, finally, do we turn sight to insight?

Try it again without the commas: How finally do we turn sight to insight?

I am beginning to see that the method of metaphor, the ability to achieve functional unity between two quite distinct images, leads in its own way to a kind of stasis. It can be a process of negation as surely as it is a process of affirmation. Indeed, it leads to a kind of neutrality.

In this respect the method of metaphor lies at the center of Eastern thought as a means of relieving the otherwise irreconcilable tensions among all manner of differences in temporality, materiality, character, personality. It is the method of mysticism. It is the hung jury. It is in one aspect, therefore, the ability to hold the world in abeyance, to stop the clock, to have it both ways, to authenticate paradox.

But in its other aspect, metaphor may be seen as the denial of animal being, the inability to make a decision of consequence, the personal abdication from the need to make inevitable choices. Because it idealizes balance and denies contrariety, it produces only potential and not actual dynamics. In the ultimate metaphor, nothing happens— everything *is* (or *is not*). Nothing becomes. It is pure conception: In its extremity, it cues no action.

Whenever his or her work has become a religion rather than a way or an occupation, the poet in Western culture has typically become an outsider. He or she has tended to become disoriented from the humanity that poetry proposes to speak for, has tended more and more to enter the realm of metaphor and to leave the "practical" world of analogy. This may be the poet's chief distinction among us. When the lay person asks, "What do you do?" and is told, "I write poetry," the response is typically disturbing. It should be. That is not what was asked, and the lay person is likely to frown and ask again, "But what do you *do?*"

Even fiction or any "creative" writing is to some degree suspect since there is apparently (or even *actually*) no issue involved, no product for one's labor. The poem, the story, the creative essay has no corporeality, no substance, except figuratively. It is made of words. Probably the only answer that makes analogical sense is that the literary artist writes *books*. The books are his or her products. That they are filled with words and thus reduce to nonmaterial and unfulfilled metaphor is nevertheless still true. To the unsophisticated, they are still *make-believe* and acceptable only as such.

Here is the danger, as it strikes me now. The poet who pursues metaphor alone also pursues indecision and madness. The world is not idea although for centuries it has been a compelling idea to think so. The world is primarily active and only reflectively fictive.

For purposes of reflection, though, or of meditation (which has to do with thought in the middle of things), the metaphorical imperative remains our human distinction, one's way to get beyond ourselves, the basis of our vision even more truly than the physics of the eye. Idea is, at its purest, a species of metaphor that holds the world in abeyance. The danger, again, is that it holds the person who has the idea in abeyance as well. Just as pure metaphor becomes stasis, pure idea is death—noncorporeal existence. This has to do with spirit, with nonmortality. It is clearly the stuff of what we have thought of, until now, as religion and theology.

But if it is to affirm and feed life rather than to negate and starve it, the revelation of metaphor must always return to the world of act. The vision must have its consequence. It must be related to—and in—the human drama. Disembodied poetry has no apparent consequence. To the Western mind, therefore, it is illusion.

The trouble with poetry in this respect is that it can come to cultivate the qualities of words for the words' sake, and words themselves are metaphors. This is quite unlike art for art's sake in the other media. The painting or art object, regardless of whether it is representational or nonrepresentational, rational or irrational, becomes an object. It occupies space and assumes its corporeal, spatial reality. In like fashion, although rather more mysteriously because of the nature of its medium, music assumes physical reality and existence by occupying time, and time, like space, is of course one of the dimensions or grounds of reality. Not so the metaphor transmitted in words, *unless we are equally aware of the poem, the novel, the book of words as art objects, filling space with significant form, and as sound, like music, occupying time.*

Robert Frost referred to a poem as "a momentary stay against confusion"; yet the essence of metaphor *is* confusion.

SQUARING THE CIRCLE
or
On the Road to Mandala

The contradiction can be understood only . . . as a visual
representation of the mathematically insoluble problem of
the squaring of the circle, which had greatly preoccupied the
Greeks and was to play so great a part in alchemy. . . . The
circle is a symbol of the psyche. The square is a symbol of
earthbound matter, of the body and reality. In most modern
art, the connection between these two primary forms is
either non-existent or loose and casual. Their separation is
another symbolic expression of the psychic state of 20th-
century man.

—Aniela Jaffe

*   *   *

As the geometer who bends all his will
    To measure the circle, and howsoe'er he try
    Fails, for the principle escapes him still,

Such at this mystery new-disclosed was I,
    Fain to understand how the image doth alight
    Upon the circle and with its form comply.

—Dante, "Paradiso"

*   *   *

1

Angles corner everywhere I look;
the shapes of tables, chairs,

133

windows, walls—whole houses
box in squares.

Notwithstanding this, I'm told
that cosmic space is curved, that
out beyond our earthbound sight
no fate is flat.

2
A missile arches into space and
into orbit by going straight;
power gone, the gravity of spheres
must compensate.

Placed within the courtly lines
that mark their boundaries,
tennis players stroke the ball
with circular ease.

3
Me? I stand up straight and
square my shoulders; still I find
I undulate and have to trust my
curvature of spine.

I sense the curve of cosmic time
implied in every common act;
the broken bowl remains in shards
a concave artifact.

4

Maybe the circle's curve prevails
despite the angular forms we build
with lumber, plastic, steel—despite
the world we've willed.

But even so, I need my rigid
mortal frame of mind to mark
how even the level human eye
describes an arc.

This perspective, then:

The practical world—that world in which we must live together with our differences, with the world's differences—is the world of analogy. It is the world of likeness and difference spelled out, of potentially infinite variety, but also of accessibility by way of analogical teaching and learning. This is the world into which we are born, in which we learn to make decisions and to act. (Curiously, it does not seem to be the world into which we die.)

Equally essential to our humanity, though, is *the metaphorical imperative*—the human dimension of idea in which there can be unity; in which there can be a standoff between alternatives, a "perfect" ambiguity; in which all things are possible and are apparently of no consequence.

The tendency of Eastern thought, psychology, and religion has been toward the metaphorical existence, toward making the practical, analogical, active life illusory and insufficient. The West, on the other hand, has struggled to affirm the practical, analogical, active life by holding firm to dualities that set the metaphorical state (religion, hope, irrationality) over against the analogical state (secularity, acts, reason). The nagging difficulty in human history over the centuries has been the lack of a vital pertinence of these two states to each other—the difficulty in having the creative and the maintenance functions working together, so to speak.

A world that neglects the metaphorical imperative is subhuman. A world that insists on a metaphorical reality without relevance to the analogical method is superhuman. To insist on either without the balancing component of the other is to deny humanity its way, to fail in the need to know ourselves and to succeed ourselves.

Those hauntingly whole photographs of our planet from space are really portraits, the most up-to-date portraits available, of *us*, the first complete group photographs we've ever had.

I can't see myself in them, of course, but I can't help feeling as personal about them as if I could. So *that's* how I look from "out there"! (Ah, to see ourselves as others see us.)

Those photographs present an image that I *believe*, in both their explicit and implicit disclosures. Though unseen, Clam Lake, these winter woods, and I are in those photos, and this fact provides me with a new metaphysical realization I cannot escape: I see myself first from my own limited mortal view here in my immediate surroundings, with my customary horizontal vision stopped by the log walls of the cabin and, beyond them, by the encircling line of my earthbound horizon. Simultaneously I see and accept myself in this new image of the wholeness of the detached globe we call Earth, on which gravity permits me to stand. This second image is as valid for me as the first. My identity is confirmed by both images conceived together although in nearly all respects, such as distance, size, position, and perspective, they are contradictory. It is a religious experience.

The role of humility before one's God in the old theistic religions becomes in our time the humility we feel before our growing awareness of the limitless complexity of things—we ourselves, paradoxically, being the most complex of all.

If we are to sustain and extend life on this planet rather than destroy it, we must accept, with the faith and fervor that has until now been channeled into our formal religions, the paradox of our origin and our position: While we come more and more into control of our immensely complex planet and its vital ecological balances, we remain as much as ever an integral part of its vulnerable organic systems.

What do I really know of my relationship to the things of this Clam Lake winter world? How much a part of them have I become?

Is my learning to take them for granted, to *assume* them in their places, I in mine, an advance in perception or a retreat?

Does habit necessarily dim special awareness of the world around us? How does *habit* fit into *habitat?*

It is sometime before dawn, and I have been awakened by a mysterious confluence of sounds in the night and words in my mind. I have no clear notion of what the sounds were although my experience through so many long Clam Lake winter nights suggests any number—an owl's hollow hoot, the wail of a coyote, a fox's sharp bark, a passing timber wolf's howl, the groan of the ice shifting on the lake, the scuttling of a mouse along the shelf paper in the kitchen, or the same miscreant caught in the wastebasket and vainly scrambling to get out, the cracking of trees in the intense cold, even the inexplicable creaking of logs, floorboards, and joists in the cabin, or the soft click and hiss of dying embers in the fireplace as they break and fall into a cooling bed of ashes. Perhaps a rising wind. Perhaps a sudden drop into silence at its cessation.

About the words, though, I have no trouble remembering: *common ground*. They stuck in my head at that instant and turned there through so many enlightened permutations—almost simultaneous—that they put behind me any chance of further sleep. *Common ground*. The words seemed so insistent, so portentous, so clear, that I got up, despite the cold and the unlikely hour, dressed as hurriedly as I could, and after laying and lighting a hasty fire, sat blinking at the table to follow the unbidden calling, the promise, the peculiar mandate that had roused me so suddenly and fortuitously in the dark.

I press for recollection, for that initial link that can connect me again with the whole chain of perceptions, but it is elusive and pulls back. *Common ground*. It somehow contained all the principles of life and death and vivid thought in between. I'm almost embarrassed to recall that moment since it held such confirmation as defies elucidation. I may not be able to retrieve it whole, to bring it back entire, but maybe I can search around the pieces, although the full silence of the night and the flickering of the firelight begin to mock me, and I fall into some doubt of my own wits, of what I had accepted in that half-awake state as my own prescience. *Common ground.*

One sidelight I do recall—an ironic note—that in one sense the winter itself has denied me common ground in these woods by blanketing all with snow and ice. Unlike the year-around creatures with whom I share the neighborhood, I have not yet walked the land. Instead, I have been walking on air, on the insulating layers of crystallized moisture condensed from the transient winter skies and spread over the forest floor and the sleeping lake.

Still there is the compelling echo of wholeness in the phrase that held my mind, an echo of the revelation bringing together earth, air, water, rock, and fire with all the life phases they have together engendered. And the death phases as well, which I knew to be arrival as much as departure.

How much time gone by—a half-hour? An hour? No matter. The moment of illumination has gone, and I am left with only the glow and the words. Maybe the dictionary can stir them up and get me back on the track.

> *common:* of or relating to a community at large; public; shared by two or more individuals or by all members of a group; familiar; widespread, general; characterized by a lack of privilege or special status; a piece of land subject to common use.
> *ground:* earth, soil, dirt; land, property, terra firma, real estate; basis, foundation, substructure, matter, substance, material; reason, cause, motive, footing,

origin, beginning; a fundamental logical condition; a basic metaphysical cause; an object that makes an electrical connection with the earth.

Common ground. Well, why not? If God is dead, he should at least have a proper burial: File him in our ancestral plot—under *ground.* One with the diurnal cycles of Earth. God become *humus* —"a complex variable material resulting from the partial decomposition of plant and animal matter, and forming the organic portion of the soil." Deity metamorphosed—recycled—into substratum. Common Ground. The Ground of our Being.

Here I sit, staring at the page and at the crackling fire, quite warm now. Looking out the window into the depth of the night, I see my reflection in this glowing room suspended in the surrounding darkness, waiting for the black beyond my reflection to show the first dusty dilution of approaching dawn, then the imperceptible shades of gray lead to faint rose, the growing promise of the sun, and the heralded break of day. The images grow, and the words dwindle.

At least with respect to the bear who shares my locale, my intuition is sound. Today as I walked through the snow-filled woods just a few hundred yards from the cabin, I discovered where he sleeps away our Clam Lake winter. A mound of snow against the bank of a small hill caught my eye, for a faint mist of steam was rising from it into the sun-bright air. I had never seen this effect before, and for a moment I wondered why the conditions did not produce such steam over the whole snow surface. Why steam only in this one spot?

Then I realized that the cause lay beneath the surface. I had located my bear. Under four or five feet of snow and curled into the round of the burrow he had dug into the side of that small rise, he slept on. Reduced as his body heat was in his deep winter coma, it was sufficient under the particular conditions as I passed by today to cause that slight steam and to mark his place.

For an instant I considered clearing away enough snow to get a look at him, but I abandoned the impulse just as quickly. Instead, I stood there looking intently at the spot for some time. The steam continued to rise from the surface, and I visualized that huge shaggy ball of black bear beneath the mound. He was there. I turned away and walked back to the cabin, leaving him to sleep away the rest of his winter.

FEBRUARY POEM

I am a hungry hibernating bear
Curled around my leather paws.
Now and then I growl
Within my torpid sleep
As bearish images of summer
Circulate their sunlit urges
Through my sluggish winter blood.
My dreams are full of woods

And honey, grubs and roots.
I growl within my hungry sleep.
My tongue licks out between my teeth.
I want to prowl. I want my heat.

Fr. *métaphore*; L. *metaphora*; Gr. *metaphora* < *metapherein*, to
carry over; *meta*, over + *pherein*, to carry.

Winter has no entrails. At its heart is an echo.

My dear Lueders:

In a day or two I will leave. I have used your property long enough. I have about finished what I came for, that is I have found it cannot be finished, and I am satisfied with that.

The snow still lies deep in your woods. It will be months before you return to the cabin. I have run onto things while I was here, and I have run out of things—like food. Either way, it is time to move on.

I am sorry your food has been depleted. It really bothers me to see your supplies getting low and to know I can do nothing about it. I can't pay you back in food. There is no way for me to replace the gas and electricity consumed. One way or another, though, everything I have used here is a part of what I have written out. I have decided therefore to leave all my writing here when I go. I leave it to you.

Like the wood rat, I have my own measure of value, my own way of keeping ledgers. I refer you, Lueders, to the entry describing that creature on page 64 of your copy of **American Wild Life Illustrated,** *compiled by the Writers' Program of the Works Progress Administration in the City of New York, published by Wm. H. Wise & Co., Inc., 1946:*

The animal lives in wooded and swampy
areas where plague germs are not met

with as frequently as in the sewers
and cellars inhabited by its introduced
cousins. . . .

    This creature comes by its
additional names, trade rat and pack
rat, because of its mercantile traits.
Whereas most rats and mice simply
appropriate goods outright, the wood
rat replaces the commodity with what
it judges to be a fair amount of
some other goods. It will swap rice
for collar buttons as readily as
collar buttons for rice.

I trust you will prefer, along with me, the habits of the pack
rat to those of its reverse, the rat pack. If the exchange of my
collar buttons for your rice seems unequal, that is merely one
way of looking at it. In any event, I have taken the rice, and
you have the papers, and that is that.

    What I needed to do at your cabin was to lengthen and
coax my thought, to write whatever I would write and not to
judge or arrange it for others. I leave that option to you,
Lueders. My current needs have been served, and I shall be
moving on. For one thing, your electric blanket is an ingenious
improvement over the pile of covers, but in the long run it is
more satisfactory than satisfying. There are better ways to
stay warm at night. And I weary of talking to inert paper, to
the vapid TV, to an absent host—none of which has body or
talks back to me. In short, my need now is for companionship.
I am ready to mix in the worlds of others again. Language, I
find, is a social rather than an individual enterprise.

EPILOGUE

I am sensible of a certain doubleness by which I can stand as remote from myself as from another. . . . When the play—it may be the tragedy of life—is over, the spectator goes his way. It was a kind of fiction.

—HENRY D. THOREAU, *Journals*

Suddenly I saw he was more real to himself than I am to myself, and that what was required of me was to experience this reality of his not as an object but as a subject—and *more* real than mine.

—DAG HAMMARSKJÖLD, *Markings*

And behold, thou wert within me, and I out of myself, when I made search for thee!

—SAINT AUGUSTINE

God wrote it.   —HARRIET BEECHER STOWE, of *Uncle Tom's Cabin*

EPILOGUE

At the risk of backtracking, I would like to indicate in a more extensive way the course and result of my attempts to discover the identity of the author of the Clam Lake Papers. But despite my wishes in the matter, and my diligence, there is little I can report beyond what has already been provided.

In my questioning of the year-around residents of Clam Lake—including Pearl Accola, who writes the "Clam Lake News" column for the weekly *Glidden Enterprise*—I was unable to develop any leads that might take me farther toward identifying the author. During the winter months, they reported, there had been the usual straggle of transients—hunters, off-season tourists, snowmobilers, and skiers on their way to Mt. Telemark or other winter sports areas along the Gogebic-Penokee

Range, east toward Hurley. None had apparently stayed more than a few days or repeated their visits to town. Lacking even the slightest bit of physical description, I was at a loss to pursue my line of questioning.

Chances are, as I came to realize increasingly while working over the Papers, their author will remain unknown. Willfully, he withdrew at the end of his season without any signature on the written words he left behind, without promise or threat regarding the future that might lead us to suppose he would appear again in our midst.

I have many times wished at the very least to know his name. One wants an image too and perhaps will have it in spite of all. Through my editorial involvement with the Clam Lake Papers I have formed my own picture of their author, but I should not in the least be surprised if my picture could never be duplicated by anyone else, for that is clearly in the nature of the situation.

Finally, then, I can only report that the author has in fact returned to his anonymity and oblivion—at least far enough beyond the scope of my cabin at Clam Lake so that his person is at large and lost to me. I have to keep reminding myself of two realities, as it were: First, I didn't know him prior to his winter presence in my cabin; second, even if I should meet him face to face in the days to come, unless he chooses to reveal himself to me, I shall have small means myself of recognition. I should not know him from Adam.

EDWARD LUEDERS
Clam Lake, Wisconsin